My
Chinese Babies

Florentine Kay

Published by: Florentine Kay
Copyright ©2008 Florentine Kay
Coverdesign by Albert Jan
ISBN 978 0 9563360 0 2

*Dedicated to all the Chinese babies
who have crept into my heart
and have given me such joy*

Introduction

In 2007 I spent a year volunteering in China, for an American foundation that takes care of abandoned children with medical conditions. This experience to me has been more enriching, fulfilling and rewarding than anything I have done before in my life. Or than I could have possibly imagined it would be before I left. During this year I had the opportunity to learn a great deal about paediatric medical care, institutional care, Chinese culture and language, China's abandoned children and how the system deals with it, not to mentioned befriending numerous amazing people and making a small difference in the lives of many children.

Originally it had been my intention to write an anthropological work about the abandoned babies in China after returning. To try and explain to people where the abandonment stems from and how it is dealt with. However I have come to see that I do not have nearly enough information to undertake such a project. This is an insight I have gained mostly from reading other researchers' accounts, published only after many years of research, some of whose findings go directly against what I have personally witnessed in China. I suppose China is too vast a country to allow any general statements to be made about it.

So I have decided to limit myself to recounting some impressions of my personal experiences during my year in China. This book is written partly for myself, to gather my thoughts about the experience while writing. Secondly it is written for those who are interested to know what happened to me during that year. An answer to the many questions I have been bombarded with both during my stay and after my return.

The first part of the book will consist of brief theoretical background to my work in China. I find that without explaining something about the way the care system at the foundation works, and some knowledge of the political background in the areas I lived and worked, it is hard to get a real idea of the situation. I hereby acknowledge that while the situations described are strictly true, they cannot be taken as the general conditions in China.

One of the reasons why I cannot make general statements about China is that I have never visited the south of China. Which I know from many accounts to be vastly different from the cities in the north and central areas of China that I have lived in.

I would like to warn readers that this book is not written for those with a weak stomach or tender nerves. While I maintain that my overall impression of my experience in China was resoundingly positive and that I myself was initially surprised at how strongly the happiness of the children outshone everything else. Things – mostly relating to medical situations – did happen and will be described which some people may find too graphic for their taste. Even if I do try to keep medical details to a minimum. For those who are interested I have given a lay woman's explanation of the medical conditions mentioned in the medical glossary at the back of the book.

It has taken me long and hard thinking before I finally decided not to write this work under my own name. I stand for what I write. However there are other things to consider.

To start with, while everything written here is my personal experience and opinion, some of it is not flattering to the Chinese Government and they usually do not appreciate criticism. I would very much like to be able to revisit China, to look up good friends and see some of the children again. Unfortunately it is still the case that by criticising the Chinese Government one risks being blacklisted. For this reason I would appreciate it very much if anyone who is aware of my real identity or who manages to discover it, would not share this knowledge with others.

Even more important to me, however, is protecting the foundation I worked for. They are doing fantastic work, helping hundreds of children, and it would be terrible if this would be put to an end because of their affiliation with a 'rebel' like myself. So I will neither reveal their name, nor mine, nor the locations where they have their children's homes. To still allow the reader to make sense of which place I am talking about at any given time, I will use their relative geographical locations as designations.

EAST being the largest location, the medical and administrative centre of operations, in a large city in the east of China. WEST the second largest, located in a provincial capital in central China. NORTH next in line, an industrial city in the North of China. And finally SOUTH, only opened towards the end of 2007 in a small town in the mid-west of China.

While I spent time at all of these locations, most of my time was spent living in WEST, a total of eight and a half months. I have many times called it *wo zhongguo laojia* 'my Chinese home of origin'. Leaving there was the hardest thing I have had to do all year.

'So why did you leave?' I have been asked many times. Especially since there have been attempts to keep me. There were several reasons not to stay beyond the year agreed to at the start. The two main reasons where:

1) While I thoroughly enjoyed my time in China and felt privileged to be able to do what I was doing, I did not have the desire to settle in China, to stay there for several years. A similar feeling as that which I had after living in Denmark for a year and a half. Making the leap from one to several years would have been a logical consequence. The positions I have been offered there were all positions which should only be accepted with the intention of staying in them for a considerable amount of time. Since high turn over of management staff is not good for the children.

2) The kind of work I did, required giving your all. When it comes to the lives of small children, you really cannot give less than that. At least I cannot. As I accumulated more knowledge and was able to be of more service, this led relatively quickly to my working seven days a week and being on call at all times. This was not imposed on me. It was my own choice. Something like this I am incapable of doing by halves.

Unfortunately in consequence I knew I would only be able to do it for a limited amount of time, before I would run myself into the ground.

The combination of these reasons has led me to the decision to leave it to exactly the year. While I never at any point regretted the decision I made, I was very well aware that it would be hard to leave, and it was. The problem is that you decide to go and stand by that decision, but 'not just now'. 'Now' is never the right time, and it never will be. I realised that in advance, so I left myself no option. I did not renew my visa, so I had to leave the country before it expired.

Now that I have answered one of the most heard questions, I should answer one more, before getting to my story. That question of course being: 'How did you decide to go to China for a year?'

The answer to that question goes back a long time. From when I was very young, I had a fascination with China. But only the old China. Communist China did not attract me at all. So I did not really have any intention of actually visiting the country, since I saw it as 'completely ruined'. As a teenager I went through a phase where I desperately wanted to learn to read Chinese. For some reason speaking it, did not hold any appeal to me at the time. This never actually happened, but at fifteen there was a year where I ate almost exclusively with chopsticks.

At the age of seventeen, I saw a documentary about a home in Hong Kong where abandoned baby girls were taken in and cared for. This appealed to me tremendously. Being very much into taking care of babies, sometimes babysitting 5-6 nights a week, I thought I would really like to do something like this. However at the time I had neither the experience, the money, nor the courage to undertake something like that. The idea faded into the background, but never disappeared completely.

About ten years later I was in a call-centre job, which frustrated me to no end. This because of the horribly senseless work, and the inhumane way the company treated its employees. One night in June I watched another documentary dealing with abandoned girls both in China and in India. Suddenly everything came together. The thought I had at seventeen of doing something like that, the anthropologist in me who still had not spent any significant amount of time outside of Europe since being awarded her MA - or before that, for that matter, the call-centre agent in desperate need of getting out of her job and doing something meaningful, the linguist spotting another language learning opportunity, and so on. In short that same evening I decided I would go to China for a year. I gave myself a couple of months to mull the idea over in my head, but nothing changed, I was going.

Then came the job of finding an organisation to volunteer with. Which is a lot harder than it sounds. I spent two whole days looking around on the internet. You really would not believe how hard it is to find a volunteer organisation that does not charge you absolute fortunes, sometimes as much as several thousand euro a month, rarely less than a thousand a month, to be allowed to work for them without getting paid. Apart from point blank disagreeing with this on principle - I am willing to donate my time, work and pay for my own flight and other necessities, but that is as far as it goes, I also quite simply do not have that kind of money. I was already saving hard to get flight tickets, visas, vaccinations, etc. arranged.

In the end I stumbled across the foundation I ended up with. Who, when I said I would stay for a year, asked for no fees and even offered free room and board. So months of preparations began and at the start of 2007, I got on a plane to China.

PART 1   THE SYSTEM

Abandonment

That China has a one-child-policy in place, is known pretty much all around the world. As is the fact that this policy has caused a lot of girl-babies to be abandoned or even killed. A slightly smaller group of people will also be aware that Deng Xiaoping brought in the official one-child-policy in 1979. However both in my time in China, through stories of people and things I have witnessed, and after I returned during the reading of books related to the subject, I have learned a lot of things connected to the one-child-policy that I had never heard of. I am likely not to be the only one.

For instance it is true that Mao Zedong encouraged the forming of large families in the 1950s and 1960s, and that after his death it was Deng Xiaoping who started the strict one-child-policy. However the lines are not clear-cut. At the start of the 1970s, when Mao Zedong was still firmly in power, a two-children-policy already emerged, which just like the later one-child-policy was enforced very strongly. [Mosher p116-117]

Later, while couples were officially allowed to have one child, they could not just have one whenever they felt like it. Before getting pregnant, they needed to obtain a quota for a specific year, and then they could try and get pregnant. This quota was only valid for that particular year. If the couple did not conceive in time, the quota was of no use anymore. Just like second or higher parity pregnancies were subject to forced abortion, an illegal first pregnancy – one without a quota – would also be terminated if discovered. [Mosher p169-171]

It is widely known that very strong coercive measures are taken to implement the one-child-policy. More and more reports from witnesses are coming out in the west. However officially Chinese still maintain that this is not the case.

'The Chinese Government has always emphasised that family planning is to be carried out by the people on a voluntary basis, and not by coercion. In the meantime, it has conducted propaganda among the people about the importance of family planning (…). The propaganda is also directed towards the protection of female babies and the protection of women who gave birth to them from discrimination. (…) The Chinese people have come to understand that population growth must keep pace with the country's economic and social development and that family planning is by no means only a personal affair, but also an important matter affecting national prosperity and the people's living standards and cultural level. They have actively responded to the call of the government and voluntarily practiced family planning.' [Zhai p86]

This is a quote from someone from the Institute of National Studies at the Chinese Academy of Social Sciences in Beijing, in a publication made when he visited the University of Leiden in Holland. From what I have seen and read myself, I would say those 'actively responding' are mostly those who are charged with enforcing the policy, rather than the people themselves.

One of the new bits of information that surprised me most was that while the international community is currently relatively uniform in condemning the one-child-policy and the way it is implemented in China. In 1983 China was awarded the UN Population Award, the first to be awarded. This symbolises the UN's approval and encouragement of the Chinese family planning program. [Zhai p83]

The current one-child-policy is no longer strictly that everywhere in China. For a start, the one-child-policy only applies to Han Chinese, the ethnic majority in the country. Minorities and foreigners – also if only one of the parents is foreign – are exempt. Then because the one-child-policy was leading to the disappearance of such a high number of female babies that problematic sex ratios were coming into existence, especially in the country side, in a lot of places the policy was relaxed to a 'one-boy/two-children-policy'. Meaning that if your first baby is a girl, in certain areas you might be able to obtain permission to try again. [Kay Ann Johnson pxviii-xx, p59]

While the abandonment of girls reflects very badly on women's status in society, I would like to bring forth a few mitigating circumstances. First of all while it certainly seems true that by and large women are seen as a somewhat lower class of human than men in China, their status is been raised considerably over the last century. The Communist Party has worked hard at this. For a very long time, through much of Chinese history, they were barely regarded has human at all. Female infant abandonment is not a new thing. What is new is that now it happens under pressures put on the population largely by the government.

    Most people do not abandon their girl because they do not want the girl. Generally she is abandoned because the family want a son. Which is not the same thing. It is becoming clear that people in China increasingly feel that the ideal would be to have one of both. [K.A. Johnson p87-89] The problem is that a man is needed to carry on the family name, something that weighs quite strongly in large parts of what we call the Western World as well. There is also the fact that traditionally when a man and a woman marry, the woman moves in with her husband's family. In fact the obligation of a son to look after his parents is included in the Chinese constitution. The consequence of this, in a society that strictly enforces a one-child-policy, is that if you have a son, you will automatically gain a daughter, once he marries. If you have a daughter, you will lose her to her husband's family and will be left with nothing. Who, then, will look after you in your old age, in a country where for most people children are their only pension?

    Not everyone who has too many children – which in most cases means girls, because they keep trying to have a boy – abandon their babies. Though very rare, there are families of three, four and even five children in China. If a couple has somehow managed to not be discovered until after the baby is born, they can keep the baby. However once they are discovered to have 'over quota' children, they are fined extremely heavily. Sometimes as much as a year's salary or more. Their child will not be entitled the normal health and other allowances, which the state provides for single children. The parents also risk not being promoted in their job, being demoted or even losing their job, and forced sterilization. In order to avoid being discovered, some parents choose not to register their baby, leaving their own birth child without a *hukou* and thus a 'black child'. [K.A. Johnson p120-122]

I once found myself in a situation where we were trying to resuscitate an abandoned, newborn baby in the street. We were soon surrounded by quite a crowd who were commenting on the situation, asking questions and giving advice. Standard in newcomers was the question: is it a boy or a girl? Only when the answer turned out to be 'boy', did the question come up: why would parents just abandon it?

It is not socially acceptable, but it is a culturally acknowledged fact that girls are abandoned for being girls, while with boys there has to be another reason. We don't know why this little boy was abandoned. He did not make it. And we don't know whether he died as a consequence of being abandoned, or whether his parents abandoned him because they were told of some condition he had.

Another interesting aspect of the case of this little boy was the way the authorities handled it. It was not a baby who came from a state-run orphanage. A lady had heard of our children's home and wanted to leave the baby, which she said she had found in a hospital, with us. For reasons, which I will explain later on, we were unable to accept the baby 'off the street' like that. So we advised the lady that she needed to follow proper procedures and call the police, who would take the baby to an orphanage.

She did this. However since the baby was very small and weak, we provided all the care we could while waiting for the police to arrive. We gave the baby oxygen and wrapped him up with hot water bottles to raise his body temperature, which was very low. We waited for the police for an hour and a half. Despite repeated phone calls made, also by helpful bystanders, who stressed the fragile state of the baby every time. In the end the baby died, despite attempts to resuscitate him, five minutes before an ambulance arrived.

Initially the ambulance staff refused to even look at the baby, when we told them he had passed away. Eventually they were persuaded to confirm our diagnosis. Then the police arrived and the police and the ambulance staff fought for several minutes over who was to take the dead baby with them. They broke up for a while, with the matter undecided. When the policeman had his back turned, the ambulance tried to take off, and was stopped again. Another heated discussion, and finally the ambulance left, with permission, without the baby.

Statements were taken, and the lady who had found the baby was taken away in the police car, holding the dead baby. In the days following, we got several visits from the police, mostly connected with my presence – a foreigner – on the scene.

The abandonment of girls we hear a great deal about. Books have been written, documentaries have been made, and all about the plight of the Chinese baby girl, who is abandoned. About the orphanages filled to the brim with healthy baby girls. They and the rare, occasional handicapped baby boy, who is mentioned barely in a whisper, before moving rapidly on.

Imagine my surprise when I arrived in China to start caring for these poor abandoned foundlings, and found that more than fifty percent of the children in the care of the foundation were boys. Sometimes well over fifty percent. At one point, for quite some time, we had three girls out of 16 babies in the WEST baby-home. All baby boys, mostly dressed in girls' clothes, because the generous people donating the clothes all presumed, like most of the world, that an abandoned Chinese baby equals a girl.

Now of course, one explanation is that we were taking care of children with medical conditions, which would automatically bring those 'rare, occasional baby boys' to our door. But this could not be the whole answer. After all, from the way they are discussed in the different media, even unhealthy boys are extremely rare in the orphanages. So how was a single orphanage able to supply us with sometimes as many as three or four newborn baby boys in a single week. From what I had heard, they would barely get as many as that in half a year. Then when I visited an orphanage, I did not find the rows and rows of cribs filled with healthy baby girls, which ought to be there to balance out the 'few' baby boys.

Someone told me, when I had been in China a few months, that in the south of China mostly healthy baby girls are abandoned, while in the North of China the majority of abandoned babies are boys with medical problems. I have never been able to research this and test whether it is true. However when I compare sex ratio in the data from the media, which for the most part, does in fact come from orphanages in the south of China, and that in the population of foundlings that we received not from one, but from six orphanages in the North of China, it does seem to have some foundation.

What is the main reason behind the abandonment of these babies, both boys and girls, with medical problems? I have discovered several reasons. One is the Chinese medical system, which is greatly feared by a lot of people, and not entirely without grounds, as I will discuss in a later chapter. From what I experienced in China, I do not believe that there is an inherent, cultural aversion to people with handicaps. I have seen many people in the streets with facial deformities, skeletal deformities and other handicaps, who simply went about their lives and were treated as any other. The interesting thing was, however that all these people were above the age of thirty. In other words they were all born before the one-child-policy came into effect.

When a child is severely handicapped, be it physically or mentally, and you are only allowed to have one child, the same problem arises as in the case of girl babies: Who is going to take care of you in your old age? Or for that matter, who is going to take care of the child once it has grown up and cannot look after itself?

Then there is another reason, which I believe to be real, even though it is easily overlooked: Abandonment as an attempt to save a baby's life. Especially in the case of babies with a cleft lip and palate, I have heard many times, both from Chinese and from foreigners the comment: 'Why would you abandon a child for something like that? It only takes a small operation, it is not a big deal!'

This, if you do not mind my saying so, is very easy to say. If you have the money for the operation and access to the things you need, indeed, it is not a big deal. What people forget is that a baby with a cleft palate is usually unable to drink from the breast or from a normal nipple. The opening in the roof of its mouth prevents it from creating the vacuum needed to suck out the milk. If you use special nipples, there is no problem. But not everyone as access to these. Without these it is entirely possible for a baby to starve to death, despite the best and most loving attempts to feed it.

We have received babies barely two weeks old, with cleft palates, who had lost so much weight that you ask yourself how they managed to lose so much, in their short life. I believe it entirely conceivable that parents in desperation would abandon their baby in the hope that it will be taken care of by someone who may be able to keep it alive, when it is wasting away rapidly.

There is one more category, albeit a relatively small one, of abandoned babies, and these can be both boys and girls, usually healthy. This is the group born to unmarried mothers. Sex before marriage is very unacceptable in Chinese society. Which means that single parenthood is frowned upon severely. So severely in fact, that most single women who find themselves pregnant hardly have the option of keeping the baby. Apart from the state not allowing her to have the baby, the community around her will put her under immense pressure to 'fix the problem'.

I know a young woman who was pregnant and wanted to keep the baby. She had fled to a large city to go into hiding there. She was terrified of what would happen if her family would find her. She was even unable to have contact, let alone meet, with the father of her child, because her family was keeping an eye on him and might be able to find her through him. She gave birth to a beautiful baby girl, whom she is still caring for herself. However unfortunately she is also still in hiding.

Not all abandoned babies end up in state-run orphanages. In fact some estimates say only about 20% do. Of the remaining children a relatively large part is taken care of by informal adoption, sometimes in the sense of placing the baby in a home of friends or family who are willing to raise it. Sometimes by abandoning it on the doorstep of a family who are known to be childless and likely to raise the child. [K.A.Johnson p108-110]

Then there is a number of non-state run orphanages, which are often in the hands of religious or foreign groups. Since these institutions accept children straight off the street, they are unable to provide these children with a *hukou*. And unfortunately there is a group of babies who do not survive their abandonment. Either because they were already in a very weak condition to begin with, or because of the circumstances under which they are left.

Everyone in China knows children are abandoned, and at a certain level people understand why. However it is not an accepted practice. In fact I have often heard Chinese condemn parents who abandon their babies much more fiercely than Westerners do. Some of them allow for no mitigating circumstances whatsoever.

When people think a baby might be about to be abandoned, they can also be very proactive in preventing this from happening. One of our *ayi*, caregivers, travelled on the train from NORTH to EAST escorting and caring for a baby girl who had hydrocephalus. It was already at an advanced stage when we received this baby, and her head was quite large. Somehow people had gotten it into their heads that the *ayi* was the baby's mother and that she was planning to abandon 'her daughter' on the train.

The entire 15-hour journey the poor *ayi* was criticised and her fellow passengers – who are usually very helpful and friendly – refused to allow her to go to the toilet, for fear that she would not come back. This being a particularly timid lady, she did not say anything in her own defence and just allowed people to pour abuse over her. So while a lot of babies do get abandoned, it seems like it might not always be as easy to get away with, as it would seem at first thought.

In any case, I do not agree with those who have said to me: 'Those parents, how could they do such a thing, to abandon their own baby.' In most cases, I do not believe the parents are the bad guys. I think they are usually as much a victim of the situation and the pressure put on them, as the baby is.

Fuliyuan

Abroad people usually talk about Chinese orphanages, or the state run orphanages. However in general there are very few places where there are simply orphanages. In China orphans and abandoned babies are taken care of in *fuliyuan*, Welfare Homes. In these places everyone who has no one to look after them and is unable to look after themselves, can be taken in. Usually mostly the elderly and the very young, who have no families to look after them. They live divided over different departments of the same complex.

In 1995 an international scandal broke out when the British documentary 'The Dying Rooms' by Kate Blewett and Brian Woods was broadcast on Channel 4. It showed the miserable conditions in children's departments of the Chinese 'welfare homes'. While in China it was known, in a limited circle, what was happening in the *fuliyuan*, abroad it came as a terrible shock. An immediate measure taken by the Chinese government was to send out a warning to all *fuliyuan* not to let foreigners in anymore. This is a measure which has been relaxed a lot since then, but most *fuliyuan* directors I have encountered, are still very wary of letting foreigners into their institution.

Not everyone agrees with the image painted in the documentary. For instance Kay Ann Johnson, the writer of 'Wanting a Daughter, Needing a Son' says in her book she thinks the documentary is nothing but sensationalism. She admits that when she first visited *fuliyuan* in 1991 the conditions were not good, but this, she says, should be attributed to lack of funding and lack of staff. In her experience *fuliyuan* staff did whatever was in their power to provide children with general and medical care when needed, but simply did not have the means to do so sufficiently. Over the years she has witnessed the blossoming of a *fuliyuan* into a place where local children want to get in and join the classes.

I do not in any way wish to discredit this. In fact I am delighted to hear that *fuliyuan* like this exist and that there are places where people actually care for the children in state run institutions. I can only hope that this is the case in many more places. However the fact remains that I know for a fact this is not the case everywhere.

I saw 'The Dying Rooms' only after I returned from China. It was in China that I first heard about it and I was curious to compare conditions in the *fuliyuan* twelve years ago and now. From what I had heard what was shown in the documentary was pretty awful. I have to admit that what is shown in the documentary is not pretty. However I was shocked to realise that only one of the *fuliyuan* shown in it, the very worst, came close to what I had witnessed myself, twelve years later.

I had wanted to visit a *fuliyuan* throughout my stay, just to get an idea of what conditions there are really like. Especially after all the stories I had heard, and seeing the state of the children coming out of there, into our care. However as I mentioned before, this is still a very sensitive issue. None of us went to the *fuliyuan*, including my Chinese colleagues. We would get a call, to see if we had beds, or sometimes we would call them to let them know we had beds available and ask if they had babies. Then they would come and bring the baby to us. In order to maintain the delicate relationship, which allowed us to take care of their children, we had to tread carefully. So while I had wanted to see a *fuliyuan* on the inside, after finding out exactly how things worked, I had more or less stopped hoping that I would.

Then our director was invited to come and visit the *fuliyuan* and I was permitted to come with her. It was rather a gruelling experience, but I do not regret having gone. Something like this, one cannot imagine when one has not seen it with one's own eyes. This is an impression of the visit I wrote a couple of days after having visited the *fuliyuan*:

There are three rooms, 12 cots in a room, side by side, with just enough room in between to stand sideways. Over the sides of the cots wet children's clothes are hanging to dry. The overwhelming smell of urine, with lower undertones of mould and dirt is almost tangible. It wraps itself around you as soon as you set foot inside the door. Not even the weak human sense of smell, which so quickly phases odours to the background, is able to ignore this, not after an hour or more.

In most of the cots lie babies, or so they are called. The youngest is about a month old, but the oldest might well be two or three years old. It is very hard to say, growth and development are all stunted. Almost all are lying down, unable to sit or stand. Or perhaps they have learned that anything other than lying quietly is undesirable. Almost all those over the age of 10 months lie rocking back and forth. Their head, or their entire body. If they are not sleeping. Sores on their heads from banging against the bars of the cot. Some with their faces pressed against the bars, their neck at an uncomfortable angle. One little boy grates the paint off the bed with his teeth.

The room is very cold – and it is not yet winter, autumn has only just started. The children all have clothes on, but no socks and only the smallest are covered by a blanket or quilt. All hands and feet are cold. One little boy's feet are dark purple and icy. Clothes, bed linen, children, everything is dirty.

A boy with sores on his nose and eyes. A child of maybe two years old, able to stand, has a string tied around his leg, the other side of which is tied around one of the bars of his bed. All children, without exception, have bottoms, which are covered in big sores, blisters, purplish spots and sometimes even big open wounds, which keep reopening. Not only on their buttocks, but also on their genitalia. All from lying in their own urine and faeces. Sores on heels are common, as are heads which are flattened at the back, from always lying on them.

A lot of the children have given up reacting to touch or being spoken to. Others are still desperate to make contact. They will not stop crying or saying the one word they know from the moment you enter the room. All children are hungry, when you stroke a cheek – even of children too old to have a rooting reflex – the face will invariably turn with a desperately opened mouth looking for something, anything to eat.

A remark made about one baby being dehydrated and another having a perforated middle ear infection – observations made at a glance by someone without a medical background – are received with surprise. A baby who is weak has no chance of survival. You need to be able to drink well and fast on your own, otherwise the propped up bottle will have been removed and you will have to wait for the next round.

In the rooms there is not so much as a stool on which someone could sit while holding a child. There is no need for this. There is no time for holding children. One *ayi* looks after 10 to 20 children. Not only is she responsible for feeding and changing the babies. She also has to hand-wash all their clothes and bedding. She barely has enough time to make the babies' bottles, prop them up, take them away, and from time to time change nappies - rags tied around waists. There can be no holding of babies. Is it days, weeks or months, since the baby was last picked up off its bed? The *ayi* works 15 consecutive days, 24 hours a day, and then gets to rest for 15 days. Between two of the nurseries, there is a Spartan room with a bare bed. Since she only works 'half the month', she only gets half a month's salary: 300, - RMB. There is no time or energy to try and do more than get through the day.

Food is for those who can take it. Upstairs with the older children – three years and older – it is lunchtime. In the corridor there is a bucket with a mix of stir-fried vegetables and a stack of bowls next to it. Steamed buns to go with it. The children can help themselves. If they don't – be it because they are too small to understand or because they are mentally handicapped – well, maybe next time.

People who have visited this place regularly over the last decade or more have told me that things have improved a lot.

I am sure I will be in for accusations of sensationalism myself. But to be honest this is still a rather detached, general description. What it was really like, in those rooms, words can simply not express. Plus, you also need to bear in mind that when we visited, conditions must have been relatively good. We were invited guests, they knew we were coming.

I agree with Kay Ann Johnson that the *ayi* looking after the babies cannot be blamed, they are just doing what they can with the little means they are given. However I do not believe in the line of the poor *fuliyuan* being underfunded. From what I have seen both in this *fuliyuan* and in others, funds get to the them all right, they just do not make their way down to the children – and presumably the elderly either.

The lavish offices and conference rooms, the fleets of cars, the sumptuous meals, do not speak of an impoverished institution. In fact the government has forbidden the higher management of *fuliyuan* to go out to expensive restaurants for their lunches. So in one of the *fuliyuan* we were dealing with, they solved this problem by hiring a chef - not a cook! - to provide them with restaurant style meals in the office. Colleagues of mine were there for a meeting and invited to stay for lunch. They were presented with several meat dishes, several fish dishes and a myriad of vegetable dishes. That, to Chinese standards, is utter decadence.

Due to a collision of circumstances, I was also able to have a brief look at the insides of another *fuliyuan*, in a different part of the country. In this institute there were fewer children and the general conditions looked better. The building was much better kept, brighter, because of the large windows. And despite it being winter now, it was not as infernally cold as it had been in the other *fuliyuan* at the start of autumn. There was no horrible smell in any of the places I was and the children looked cleaner.

There was also a lot more staff. I have been told that in this particular *fuliyuan* girls, who come of age, can get a job as an *ayi*, taking care of the children who arrived after them. So here it was not a case of one *ayi* looking after 10-20 children. If anything it almost looked like there was more staff than children. However this did not necessarily lead to better care. While the basic technical care is undoubtedly better, the social care is not. The *ayi* amongst themselves have a great deal of fun and laughter and chat. But there is very little attention for the children. They are washed and changed as if they are objects on a conveyor belt.

The most heart-rending thing I saw there was a baby being given a bottle. The *ayi* stood beside the cot, holding the bottle, but standing with her back mostly towards the baby, talking and laughing with her friends. So in this case it was not a case of there being no time or staff to do the feeding. If she could stand there holding the bottle for the duration, she could also have held the baby for the same amount of time. The girl was simply indifferent to the baby. To me that is almost worse than babies being neglected because of understaffing.

One of my colleagues happened to be present when a new, small, baby was brought to this *fuliyuan*. After her experience with the other *fuliyuan* we deal with, she was favourably impressed when she saw the baby was washed straight after arriving. However then the baby was just put down in a cot and left there. My colleague offered to hold the baby a while, if the staff were too busy, and maybe give it a bottle. She was told that there was really no need, to just leave the baby where it was.

Infant mortality in the *fuliyuan* is high. For an outsider it is almost impossible to find out how high, as *fuliyuan* are allowed to issue their own death certificates. Still sometimes we would have an inkling. We would be told that they had a baby girl with a cleft lip and palate, we would accept the baby and they would tell us they would bring it the next day. The following day we might receive a blind baby boy. This was an indication that the baby had not made it through the night, and it was not a once off occurrence.

I do agree with Kay Ann Johnson that the whole experience of being abandoned can weaken a baby to the point where it has no real chance of survival anymore. In our care a relatively large percentage of deaths was also within days of accepting the baby. However this weakening was not exclusively due to abandonment. The 'care' given in the *fuliyuan* had a lot to do with it.

Coming from one particular *fuliyuan*, we could tell how long a baby had been in their care, from the state of their bottom. If the skin was completely normal, they had been there less than 12 hours. Was it severely red: no more than two days. After that the breakdown of skin and how deep the lesions were, gave us a time frame. Finding out that a baby had been in the *fuliyuan* less than two days, was always a relief. This meant that other dangerous problems such as violent diarrhoea – brought on by giving undiluted cow's milk – and dehydration were less likely to be present.

I do not believe for a second that these problems were caused by underfunding of the *fuliyuan* – although they were certainly caused by underfunding of the children's department, but that is a judgement call by the director. From what I have seen myself, I really do not see that it is anything else than a basic disinterest in the children's welbeing and whether they live or die.

For instance, we would be told to expect a baby. When towards the end of the afternoon, we would phone to ask when the baby would arrive, the answer would be they were terribly sorry, but they did not have a car available at that moment, they would come tomorrow. Sometimes this would go on for two or three days before *a* – not necessarily *the* – baby would arrive. On a few occasions, when we had a car available ourselves – usually this was out on the road, driving the foster care coordinators around, to visit children and their families – we offered to come and pick the baby up. On all of these occasions, five to six cars would be standing in front of the building. Not visitors' cars, the white *fuliyuan* cars! Apparently they did not feel like coming.

On one such occasion the *fuliyuan* had told us they had two premature babies. On the first day, they could not come for 'lack of cars'. On the second day, they said the same and we decided to go and collect the babies, since particularly premature babies would be at increased risk with every added day. This turned out to be a valid concern. We received two babies, one of whom was a premie, the other was a full term three month old, with a slight heart condition. So the other premie, it seemed, had not made it through the extra waiting day.

The premie that we did get, I noticed straight away, was dangerously cold. She was this cold, after only having been carried straight from her cot to our car, wrapped up in a thick quilt, brought by us. I lay down on the back seat of our van, stripped the baby down to her nappy and put her under my clothes, on my bare skin, together with the hot water bottles which we had brought as a precaution and covered the both of us with her quilt and my coat. When we arrived back at WEST after a 40-minute drive, the baby's temperature had reached 35.8°C. If she had been made to wait another day, or if she had been transported simply wrapped up in a blanket, she would never have made it to WEST alive.

Another *fuliyuan* is located further away. If there are no delays on the way, it is a three-hour drive to get the babies from this *fuliyuan* to WEST. Which does not, of course, mean that you should feed babies along the way. When we asked them, had they fed the baby on the road, they looked at us in surprise. Why would they? In fact, they do not bring anything with them at all, for the journey. For very small, often already weak babies three hours can be a very long time to go without food and liquids. They always arrive starved, and in summer sometimes dehydrated.

When someone of our higher management visited yet another *fuliyuan* with which we have dealings and noticed that they had a tiny premature baby, she requested that the baby be handed over to us, so that we could provide her with the care she needed. The *fuliyuan* director waved this away, there was no point, she said. Babies like that always die anyway. She did not even want to attempt to save this baby. As an aside, eventually we did convince the director to let us care for the baby and the baby is still alive and doing very well.

What I think has to be the worse case we received from a *fuliyuan* in the time I was in China, was a girl I will call Fen. We were told she had a heart condition. When we received her Fen was seven months old and she weighed 2.5kg. She was nothing but skin, bones, swollen lymph nodes, uncannily long nails and dirt. This was not because she had arrived at the *fuliyuan* like this recently. Because of the system, which this *fuliyuan* uses for naming babies, we knew she arrived there five and a half months ago, at the latest. If she wasted away like that, despite their best attempts at providing her with appropriate care, then why had they not handed her over to us much sooner?

In fact, we asked the people who brought her exactly that question. Their answer was that we never had beds. That is ridiculous. In the time that Fen spent at the *fuliyuan*, we had received more than a dozen children from that *fuliyuan* alone. So why not her? In fact we had specifically asked whether they had any babies with heart conditions, twice, during that period and they had told us 'no'.

These to me are not signs of people trying to do well but being hampered by lack of means. This is very basic disinterest. I was delighted to read Kay Ann Johnson's description of a *fuliyuan* director who knew all the children by name and played with them. I am relieved that places like those exist too. My experience has been a *fuliyuan* liaison contacting us to ask if we have a bed for a baby, who when asked about the – estimated - age and the sex of the baby, has no idea. Let alone about the medical condition or name.

Another indication of basic disinterest in the children's future – should they end up having one – is the name-giving in some places. There are two issues involved in the naming of foundlings and orphans: the surname and the given name. I have not come across a *fuliyuan* where both sides were dealt with decently yet.

For a long time all children who came through a *fuliyuan* were given the surname 'Dang' which means 'of the party', that would be the communist party, of course. This is not a regular surname. In other words, when you have this surname, you are branded for life as an orphan or foundling. Some *fuliyuan* in recent times have started using different surnames instead. Names like 'Wang', 'Sun', 'Zhao' and 'Li', these are all every common surnames, allowing the children to 'disappear' in a crowd.

Strangely enough, in the *fuliyuan* I have come across, they seem to go by the thought that you cannot have everything. The ones who take the trouble to come up with proper, nice sounding given names – which might translate into 'smile', 'snowflake' or 'willow's fragrance', are the ones who still maintain the surname 'Dang'. Whereas the *fuliyuan,* that have chosen to grant children regular surnames, assign given names by a system. In one case they use a certain character as the first syllable of the given name for a given period – often a few months – and then they add a second character/syllable presumably from another list.

This sometimes leads to very unfortunate combinations. Sometimes the two characters together form a Chinese expression. Such as the baby who was named 'the wrong time for something'. Or sometimes you suddenly hit on the name of a mythological figure connect with extreme bad luck. Whenever this baby's name was mentioned, Chinese people would – without exception – exclaim how anyone could have given a child such name.

Their record keeping leaves something to be desired too. In WEST we received a baby and when we were told his name, we had to point out that there was already a baby named exactly that, who had come from their institution. They asked if we were quite sure, which we were, the baby was in EAST at the time. Then they said they would get back to us with a new name. The baby remained nameless for 24 hours, before we received a phone call with his new name.

Working with the several different *fuliyuan*, a baby's name could tell you a lot. All of us, who were well integrated in the foundation's daily care in China, could for the most part tell which *fuliyuan* a baby originated from by looking at its name.

Medical System

As mentioned before a lot of children are abandoned for their medical condition: cleft lip/palate, spina bifida, heart conditions, premature birth, cerebral palsy, epilepsy, hydrocephalus, etc. This may be because of the overwhelming medical costs that would have to be faced, or simply the damning verdict of the doctor. Something, which also plays a major role, is the fear many people in China have for the medical system. This fear is not entirely unfounded.

For example, at one point we received a baby from a *fuliyuan* who had a heart condition. After being in our care for one day, she was going downhill fast, so we brought her to the local children's hospital to see if there was anything they could do for her. On seeing the baby, the doctor exclaimed that he knew her.

The baby had been staying in that hospital for three weeks. After the three weeks, her parents, who were not from the city, only working there, had used up every single thing they owned to pay for their daughter's hospital bills. When nothing else remained, they had no choice but to take the baby out of hospital. Apparently they had abandoned her shortly after.

To us the doctor said that there was nothing they could do for this baby. This, the parents clearly had not been told, they had been allowed to hand over all they owned to the hospital, and now they also have to live with the knowledge that they abandoned their baby. We brought the baby back with us and she died peacefully the next morning, at our children's home.

Hospitals have a reputation for taking as much money as possible, doing unnecessary tests, giving unnecessary medication. Leading to the patient reaching bankruptcy without necessarily improving in their condition. This reputation is not entirely made up. It has its grounds. It causes tremendous fear among people for the healthcare system, to the point where some refuse to have anything to do with it.

In for instance in one of the major hospitals where heart surgeries are performed, you will find parents holding their babies, crying. This is not solely because of the hardship their small baby has to go through. They will tell you that they are torn. What to do?

If they abandon their baby, they will have lost their child and feel guilty for it, always. If they don't abandon the baby, and try to give it the care it needs, they won't know if it will be enough and if the baby will survive. What they do know, is that they will lose absolutely everything. Their house, all their possessions and possibly those of other family members will need to be sold in order to pay for the surgery and care needed. And it is not certain that that will be enough to cover everything. Once the money runs out completely, care stops instantly. Supposing the baby does recover once most of the money has been spent, how are they going to look after it then?

From what I have experienced myself in various Chinese hospitals, I would say that extortionist doctors do certainly exist. However there is another side to this story, I noticed. One, which may quite possibly have to do with people only having one child and wanting the very best for it. All parents, everywhere, feel extremely frustrated and powerless when their child is ill. They very much want to feel like they are doing something to improve their child's condition. Which I think in the West is one of the reasons why antibiotics are overused to such an extreme extent.

In China people will ask for medication for everything they might have. Including essentially untreatable conditions such as the common cold, and diarrhoea. This goes for both adults and children. A particularly popular form of medication is IV treatment for any and all complaints. This you can have done at the little clinic around the corner, which will have a room with beds where rows of people, also children, are hooked up to an IV drip for an hour or two. People want to feel like they are doing something, even when nothing can be done.

Something also to be taken into account is that a doctor wants to earn a living. In the places where I have been, it was always free to get a basic check up – have your lungs listened to, mouth and throat seen, abdomen felt. A doctor does not earn anything until he or she sells you medication. Or more elaborate, technical tests.

Some doctors do push this. However in my experience, a lot of doctors will suggest giving some sort of medication, but if you ask if it would be alright not to take it, they often agree. So while some physicians really do put pressure on people and will try to get every fen out of them they can grab. A lot of them are only catering to the wish of the patients. Something, which unfortunately is happening more and more in the West too.

Ironically while on the one hand Chinese doctors are feared for squeezing their patients for every Yuan they have, on the other sometimes you cannot find a doctor willing to do a certain procedure, even if you know it is possible and you are willing to pay for it. They weigh off the result of any procedure against the cost and trouble of it, before deciding to perform it or refuse to. For instance if a baby is mentally handicapped in any way, they will often not see the point and flat out refuse to perform the required treatments for physical corrections.

At times we would have to go to a great many doctors before finding one who was willing to perform the needed surgery. This takes a lot of time. Usually this means that if the surgery is performed in the end, the outcome is not quite as good as it could have been if it had been done earlier and the condition had not been allowed to run its course for quite so long.

A certain number of abandonments may probably be attributed to this as well. Cases where doctors inform the parents that there is nothing to be done for their baby, even if there might be. Quite aside from the economics.

Going into hospital in China is a completely different experience from what it is in the West. Whether you are an adult or a child, you cannot go into hospital on your own, you need someone there not just for company, but to care for your. In hospitals you need to be in with your baby 24 hours a day, otherwise it will not get basic care. Nurses are there to provide medical care, not to feed and change nappies.

Only when a baby is put in the ICU, because it is either very young or very, very weak, it is cared for by the staff. In which case you do not get to stay with the baby, or visit it. Nor in most cases will you be told anything about its condition, or be notified and allowed to see the baby if it is dying.

Not all hospitals in China are the same. Some of them have a very high standard of care and they helped a lot of the babies that passed through our hands very well. However in some places standards are frighteningly low. Even relatively 'specialised' places such as the provincial children's hospital. Provincial officially meaning most excellent of the province, but in the case that I am familiar with, the meaning is closer the first association triggered.

The one near WEST I am particularly familiar, and not too impressed with. When I first came to live out there, my instinct told me when a baby was not doing well to take it to hospital to have them look at it. As time passed and I gained more experience with the workings of this hospital, instead of being the one pushing to go to hospital, I would resist the decision, because in a lot of cases the care we were able to provide ourselves was better than what was to be expected there. Particularly after what happened to one baby we brought.

We received a newborn baby boy with a cleft lip and palate from the *fuliyuan*, not yet a week old. I will call him Shi. They told us he was doing very well, eating well, lively, etc. The first bottle we gave him, he suckled very weakly and did not manage to get much out. Just over an hour after he arrived, Shi went blue. We checked his oxygen saturation and found it was very low, so he was put on oxygen. With a feeding tube we helped him to take in the formula he needed. Over the next twenty-four hours he was relatively stable, but everything pointed towards his having a heart defect as well as the cleft lip and palate.

The next evening, we experienced a power cut. This happened from time to time, but is particularly unfortunate when you have a baby using the oxygen concentrator. We connected him to the oxygen bottle, which we had as back up. However this was almost empty, because it had recently been used to transport another baby to EAST by train. So at half past nine in the evening, our driver was called and the director, the care supervisor, Shi, I and the oxygen bottle, plus our entire collection of empty oxygen bags, were loaded into the car to go and fill everything we had up.

An hour later we returned with oxygen, and found the power had just come back on again. Shi was put back onto the oxygen concentrator, but he was moaning constantly and was clearly getting weaker by the minute. The pulse-oximeter showed that his heart rate was getting weaker and slower. He had probably been getting too little oxygen for too long. We decided to take him to hospital. So we put him back on the oxygen bottle, which was now full, and the director, an *ayi* and I rushed Shi to hospital, not sure if he would even make it there alive.

He did. We stormed into the emergency room, where a doctor came and looked at him straight away. However he pressed his stethoscope to the baby's chest for all of two seconds and gave the verdict 'pneumonia'. That was that. Then came a typically Chinese interlude. The director needed to go and pay a registration fee and get a ticket for that before anything else could be done. So the *ayi* and I were standing in Emergency with a blue baby, for whom nothing whatsoever was being done in the meantime, waiting for the formalities to be taken care of.

When the director returned, we took the baby to another wing of the hospital, where he would be admitted. There he was taken to the little examination area behind the reception desk – which is shielded from the corridor only by a large glass wall, on the other side of which a crowd quickly gathers to follow the proceedings, elbowing each other out of the way for a better view, a normal situation in many hospitals. A doctor came to listen to his chest, longer than before, at least. And another one. The baby's head was partially shaved to put in an IV and that was up and running.

While the children's home director and I explained his condition in minute detail, three times over, it took the doctors an hour and a half of intermittent listening to his chest to make the hesitant statement that Shi **might** have a problem with his heart. All of this time, he was left on the oxygen bottle which we had brought with us, which gives a less than ideal oxygen flow, just better than nothing, instead of putting him on the regulated oxygen they had available there. After finally coming to this conclusion, he was moved to one of the rooms, where after another while he was eventually placed on 'oxygen from the wall'.

Also worth mentioning is that no one ever checked his oxygen saturation. Neither to see how it generally was, nor to check whether the amount of oxygen he was receiving was sufficient. After staying with Shi for about an hour on his ward, the director and I went back, leaving the *ayi* to take care of him through the night as is usual, in our care.

The next day we were informed that Shi was scheduled for a cardiac ultrasound, on the following morning. That whole day, nothing in particular was done for him, except for the IV medication for pneumonia, which he probably did not have. That evening, twelve hours before his scheduled ultrasound, Shi passed away.

This shocked me tremendously. Not so much the fact that he did not make it, that was something we had taken into account from the moment he started going blue, shortly after he arrived. But the fact that nothing whatsoever was done for him, in a facility where they could have done something. We would have provided him with better care in our own Children's home, on his last day. Even if we could not have saved him.

After this experience, we rarely decided to bring babies in similar condition to this hospital. We preferred to care for them ourselves until they either passed away peacefully, or stabilized enough to be moved to EAST which has access to better quality hospitals.

These were not the only problems we had with this hospital. We found that when cardiac ultrasounds were performed here, the result was never the same as those gotten from the hospitals near EAST where the babies would have their actual heart surgeries. Sometimes they would spot a hole in a heart which was not there at EAST's hospitals, or would miss one which the other hospital claims was there. And if both places would agree on the existence of a hole, the size of it would invariably be different. We learned over time to put more faith in the hospitals near EAST than in the one near WEST, and children would be transported to EAST and back to get check ups in order to get more reliable assessments of their condition.

The Emergency Room in that the children's hospital near WEST was very interesting too. Children we brought in were given one of two diagnoses. Either 'no problem', or – more often – 'pneumonia'. So these cases – of babies coughing, breathing loudly or laboured etc. – we would bring to hospital for confirmation of diagnosis less and less too. We found the assessment in the clinic around the corner much more reliable. There it was also possible for babies to just have a lot of phlegm in their airways, airway infections or bronchitis, apart from pneumonia.

In the surgery department at this hospital, I do not put much trust either. On three occasions we received babies from the *fuliyuan* at WEST who were post-surgery. The surgeries had all been performed in the children's hospital nearby. All three of the babies, two boys and a girl, had been born without an anus - a condition called *anal atresia*. This is a very serious condition. In girls often there is a fistula, which allows them to pass faeces through their vagina, but boys usually have no exit to their bowels at all, which will lead to a life threatening condition within days of birth.

Usually a stoma is created, a hole in the abdominal wall, which is connected to the bowels, through this hole the faeces can pass out of the body. Then later on, when the baby is older and stronger, another surgery will be performed, where an anus is created and the stoma is closed.

In two of the babies no stoma was ever created. They proceeded to create an anus straight away. Only these were so badly done that the babies were left with a huge surgery scar over the entire width of their back. For lack of anything like a sphincter, faeces continually leaked out of their anus and ate away at their skin, despite constant monitoring and cleaning.

The third baby had in fact been given a colostomy first. But despite all of the terrible things we had witnessed before with babies coming from the *fuliyuan* we were shocked at the state of this boy's belly. One stoma had been opened, deemed unfit and largely, not entirely, closed again. Another had then been opened, which was nothing more than a hole in the abdominal wall, through which a piece of bowel was pulled out. It was sticking out more than an inch.

This baby was rushed to EAST on the first train going that way. And for a long time we did not think he was going to make it. In fact he was placed in hospice care for a while, before one last attempt to save his life was undertaken and succeeded. He is still alive today. He now has a new anus, which is hard to distinguish from a natural one and a very large scar on his belly to testify of the horrors that he has been through.

In China hospitals have in some cases different standards for when a child can undergo certain surgery. In the West there are also certain procedures which are postponed until the child is a little older and stronger, or further along in their physical development, if possible. But a lot of problems are fixed at, or very close to, birth. In China surgery immediately after birth is extremely rare. They feel newborns are not strong enough to withstand surgery. Generally speaking children need to reach both a minimum age and a minimum weight before surgery can take place. The age and weight required depends on the procedure. This can sometimes cause problems.

For example certain kinds of complicated heart surgery will not be performed until the child has reached a weight of 10kg. This weight is very hard to attain, for many children with complicated heart defects. Most children with an un-repaired heart defect are small for their age and do not gain weight easily, since most of their energy is used for keeping basic systems going. The longer the wait, the weaker the heart becomes and the less likely the outcome of the surgery is to be good. If the desired weight is attained at all, that is.

One of the most bizarre things connected with the medical system that I have encountered in my time in China, was connected with the end of life. When a baby passed away, we needed a death certificate, which we had to present to the *fuliyuan* of origin of the baby. These death certificates, we could only obtain at a hospital. And the hospital near WEST would only issue them, if the baby had died there. This led to very strange situations.

    On one occasion a baby died extremely suddenly. He had been blue and was having difficulties breathing throughout the day. He was almost ten months old, we had taken care of him almost all of his life. He had been diagnosed with tracheitis. We had been told that an excess of phlegm in his lungs was not allowing the air to pass properly that morning and in the afternoon the care supervisor and I were at the clinic around to corner to give him IV antibiotics.

    He was about half way through the IV treatment when he suddenly looked a lot better. His colour was improving and he was not moaning anymore. He looked much more alert. This lasted a few minutes, then suddenly he went downhill extremely rapidly. In the time it took us to call the doctor and for her to reach us – barely a minute – he had already passed away. Nothing could be done anymore.

    The care supervisor and I quickly wrapped up the baby in his quilt and jumped into the first taxi we saw. It took us about 45 minutes to reach the hospital through rush hour traffic. All this time we could not say anything, because the taxi driver could not know we were holding a dead baby. We could only look at one another in disbelief at how fast it had all gone.

    When we arrived at the hospital, we paid the taxi, and got out. Just outside the doors, we reattached the oxygen bag to the tube leading to the baby's nose, looked each other in the eye, took a deep breath and then ran into the emergency shouting that the baby was not breathing well and that we needed help.

Doctors came rushing over, and his chest was listened to. They checked his oxygen levels and tried resuscitation. Unfortunately, they told us, the baby had passed away. They asked if we wanted to try and revive him with more drastic measures. We acted shocked at the news – still being shocked enough about the real situation to get away with it – and said that if they were sure he was dead, there was not much point in doing anything else. So it was left at that. Which was a relief, because he had been dead for quite some time, so I was afraid if they spent too much time on him, they would find that out. After that only bureaucratic formalities had to be taken care of.

This is what was needed when a baby died outside of hospital, in order to obtain an official death certificate. It would seem comical, if it were not so tragic.

The Foundation's Care System

The WEST, NORTH and SOUTH homes have agreements with one or more *fuliyuan* in their area to take over their babies with medical conditions. Generally speaking the *fuliyuan* will call the director of the place they are affiliated with and ask if any beds are available. If there are, they will come and drop off the baby. A care-agreement is then drawn up, which states that the *fuliyuan* is still the baby's legal guardian, but the foundation is allowed to make decisions about the baby's care. From Chinese state side, effectively the baby goes into foster care when it is handed over to the foundation.

In principle, only babies from *fuliyuan* are accepted. The reason for this is that all Chinese people need to have a *hukou*, which is a personal registration number. Without this number, they officially do not exist. Children without a *hukou* are called 'black children', *hei haizi*. Without a *hukou* a person can never obtain official papers, children may have trouble enrolling in schools and international adoption is out of the question. Children, who are just picked up off the street and have not passed through the required channels, cannot get a *hukou*. So you can ask yourself whether you are doing the child a favour in saving its life and raising it, when there are no real prospects to look forward to.

The official channels to be followed at abandonment are first to report to the police, who will write a report on the circumstances under which the baby was found. Then the police will bring the baby to the nearest *fuliyuan*. At the *fuliyuan* the baby is usually checked up by a doctor, its age is estimated and it is assigned a name, a date of birth and a *hukou*.

So in WEST, NORTH and SOUTH children are accepted from the orphanages, their condition is assessed and they receive general care. EAST does not take in new children, it is the medical centre, because near its location the quality of the hospitals is higher than those available near the outlying homes. The quality of care at the local orphanages is generally also higher, so the children there are not it quite as much need of being 'saved'.

If a child is particularly weak, or when it has reached the required weight and/or age to be able to undergo surgery, they are transported from the outlying homes to EAST by train – a journey of 8-17 hours, depending on the location of origin – in the care of a caregiver, who are called *ayi*. Once a child has sufficiently recovered from surgery or general health has improved enough, they will be taken back to the outlying home they came from, again by train, by an *ayi*, to make room for other, weaker babies in EAST. In the outlying home they will continue to receive care and be monitored as long as necessary.

It is recognised that institutional care, however well organised, is not ideal for children. So as soon as their health allows and their special needs are not too complicated or delicate anymore, children are placed into local foster care families. This is not the end of monitoring their progress however. Every child is visited every week by one of the foster care coordinators, to make sure they are doing well and that the foster parents have the supplies: clothes, formula, etc., and knowledge they need to provide the child with optimal care.

Ultimately it is hoped that babies will be adopted into permanent families of their own. Thankfully a lot of them are. The foundation does not have any control over the adoption process. They are dependent on the *fuliyuan* putting the babies' files up for adoption. The way it generally works is that babies who are completely healthy – after having received the required surgery or period of care – can be adopted domestically, within China. Babies who still have special needs or deformities after they have received the surgery needed, are put up for international adoption. Unfortunately babies, who have mental disabilities, do not tend to be put up for adoption at all. While they would potentially benefit most from being adopted into a loving family.

In the children's homes, care is provided by *ayi*. One *ayi* is in charge of two children, assigned to her at the start of her shift. There are three shifts per day from 7.00 to 14.00, from 14.00 to 21.00 and from 21.00 to 7.00. *Ayi* doing dayshifts work six days a week. *Ayi* on nightshifts work two nights on two nights off. *Ayi* are not allowed to sleep at night, as round the clock care is required.

Every baby has its personal care chart, hanging on the wall. This gives name, date of birth, medical condition, special needs – including a specification for the individual child how much formula at which intervals it drinks and whether this is restricted or a guideline – and the medication it is currently on, all on the front page of the clipboard. Behind that, are sheets where the time, amount and nature of liquid and solid intake is recorded, a fever record, which gives dates, times and temperatures and a chart where the shift supervisor records and signs off on all medication when it has been given. Babies with cardiac or severe breathing problems also have a chart on which their oxygen saturation and heart and breathing rate are recorded.

On the changing table there is a chart with all the babies' names where at every nappy change the time and dirty and/or wet nappy is recorded. This allows proper, consistent care, in spite of the large number of carers. It also makes it possible to discover problems at an early stage, and when a problem is discovered, to backtrack and see where things started to change.

EAST is divided over 4 apartments with three bedrooms, each located adjacent to, or above each other and these are distinguished by the designations EAST1 to EAST4. EAST4 being a special care unit, where the most vulnerable babies are cared for. Here there are four *ayi* and a shift supervisor to six or seven babies. In WEST, and since September also in NORTH there are two apartments with children, one housing the babies and one the toddlers – the last category effectively means all children who are able to move around. Usually babies move to that home when they start crawling. SOUTH, having just started, is only one unit.

Apart from the *ayi*, every apartment has a shift supervisor, who works two twelve hour day shifts, then has two days off, then two twelve hour night shifts and then two days off again. The shift supervisor has the overall responsibility over all the babies/children in her home, assigns babies to *ayi*, oversees their care and administers medication.

When I first arrived in China, every location also had one – and EAST three, because of the larger number of children – care supervisor. These women were responsible for the basic medical care of the children. They had to check that shift supervisors were dealing correctly with medication and other special needs, they were called in first if there were possible signs of problems to assess the situation and decide what to do with it. They were supposed to keep an eye on all children to spot early signs of potential problems themselves, and explain instructions from doctors or the medical director to shift supervisors. In reorganising the care structure, this position was eliminated in EAST in spring. In autumn in NORTH because of problems with the care supervisor, she disappeared too. And in South the position was never created. So at this moment, the position only exists in WEST.

Above the carers in the homes themselves – who are all local middle class women – every location has its director, who is in contact with the orphanage and higher management in EAST, and takes care of the day-to-day running of the children's home. And every location has its foster care director and foster care coordinators, who take care of finding new foster families, screening and training them, visiting children and accompanying foster parents and children to a doctor or hospital, should the occasion arise.

In EAST there is a central management team, consisting of a medical director, who, though not a doctor, is a medically very knowledgeable person. She is called in when troubles arise at EAST, gives advise on what to do to the directors in the outlying homes, when asked, and she also organises the check ups and surgeries for all the children in the system. She is aided by medical coordinators, who take care of communication with doctors and specialist, accompanying all children, who specifically assigned to them so that there is a set contact person for each one, on hospital visits from EAST.

There is the financial director, the foster care manager, whom all foster care directors answer to, the children's home manager, whom the children's home directors answer to, and then two people who bring all of those strings together. One of whom is the CEO, the only Westerner in the whole line of employees.

While all of this was explained to me in my first days there, it did of course take me a little while longer to really make sense of both the system and of who was who. Still I was impressed with the way the babies were being cared for and the happy environment that was created for them.

One little detail which I particularly like about how the foundation works, and which I think tells you a lot about their attitude towards the children, is that unlike most foreign organisations who take in Chinese children and care for them, this one does not give the children western names. The children have already been renamed – if they were ever given a name at birth – when they arrived at the *fuliyuan*. There is no need to change their name again, for the convenience of the western visitors and workers. If you are willing to make a slight effort and have a sincere interest in the children, it is not in fact harder to learn a Chinese name than it is to learn a western one.

PART 2   MY EXPERIENCES

Arriving

Arriving in China and at the compound where EAST was located, where I would be staying for the next few weeks, was quite a shock. Not because – as everyone, including myself, expected – everything was so different. Quite the contrary. It was because I was expecting to be arriving in a completely different world and I found that everything seemed so amazingly normal. A Chinese middle class suburb, the compound consisted of apartment blocks and a little shop. Three bedroom apartments with a kitchen and two bathrooms. It all looked singularly normal. I found it hard to wrap my head around the fact that I was in fact in China.

Of course not everything was **exactly** the same. However having lived in Holland, Ireland, Denmark and France, where at first I did not expect differences, because it was after all, all Europe, I found that in the details and small things differences can be very profound. In China I was expecting everything to be completely different. Instead I found that the differences were mainly in the details and the small things.

The first few weeks I spent familiarizing myself with the working of the children's homes and trying to get some Mandarin Chinese. I had been studying on my own, with books and CDs for six months. By the time I was leaving, I have to say I was pretty impressed with my ability, in my own living room. However on arriving in China, I found I could say all but nothing and I could understand just about… nothing. Still, in management several people had English and were able to help me. While on the other hand the caregivers, who have no English whatsoever, were great because they left me no choice. If we were to communicate, it would have to be in Chinese. This was a great motivator and very effective. Although you are always mainly aware of your shortcomings, I did progress, slowly at first and increasingly rapidly.

I was quite amazed when I first went into the children's homes and saw the children there and how they were living. Before I arrived, I had this image of poor sick babies, living in essence rather miserable lives, for whom we would try and do what we could to make things bearable. What I found, could not have been a greater contrast.

The children's homes were bright and colourful, the care-giving staff plentiful and friendly and the babies very happy. All that was obvious at a glance. Of course all the babies had their medical conditions, but they do not see that as a hindrance for getting on with life, as we adults do. They are not able to compare themselves with those around them and feel they come out lacking. When they are not in pain or discomfort at this very moment, they do not give pain or discomfort a thought. They do not think about the pain they were experiencing before, or the pain, which might reappear in an hour's time. If it is not here now, it does not exist and they are happy, smiling, getting on with life.

I really enjoyed getting to know all the babies. Although it was hard at times to keep up. At the start, I was trying very hard to learn all the names, to know who was who, and who had which condition. However there is nothing static about EAST. There is no such thing as a status quo. Babies are constantly being 'swapped and changed'. Babies going in and out of hospital. New ones arriving from the outlying homes, ones I was just getting to know being send back to where they came from, because they were doing well and room was needed for weaker ones. And then there was also some moving between EAST 1,2,3 and 4.

So after about three or four weeks, I had a reasonable idea of a core group. The children who had been there most of the time I had been there. And I tried to learn as much as possible about the ones added to that every time. I divided my time between all four of the EAST homes, usually spending the hours between breakfast and lunch in one place, and then the afternoon until dinner in one of the others.

Meals are taken very seriously in China. Food in general is very important and a major topic of conversation. When I first spent my days in the children's homes, I was amazed to have babies plucked out of my arms and being forcefully 'allowed' to go to lunch or dinner by the *ayi*. Usually it started with just one, but if I did not leave soon enough, all the *ayi* present would interfere and pressurize me into leaving. Arguments of allowing a baby to finish a bottle, or letting a child in the process of falling asleep stay where it was until I could put it down in its cot asleep were all beside the point. I had to eat! Right now!

    I enjoyed the Chinese food, which was prepared for all of the management staff in an dining hall. While I did have to get used to some of the spicier foods, it never disagreed with me at all. What was very interesting to note, was that often the foreigner's present would all eat with chopsticks – something I had no trouble with, after all the practice I had had in my teens – while most or even all Chinese people present would eat with spoons.

With some of the babies I made deep connections early on, and I would gravitate to them, if they were awake while I was in the apartment where they stayed. A girl I will call Lili in particular taught me an important lesson, right at the start.

    Lili has a severe form of cerebral palsy. She is spastic, has limited use of her right arm and hand, has a seizure disorder for which she receives medication and she was unable to eat, being entirely dependent on a feeding tube to get anything into her. Mentally she is also handicapped. She was seven months old when I first met her.

    The first few times I was in EAST1 I always saw her sitting in a Maxi Cosi seat. Her arms were wrapped in restraints, to prevent her from pulling the feeding tube out of her nose. She was asleep almost all the time, breathing noisily. The rare moments when she was awake, she seemed agitated, her breathing even more noisy and someone would usually start rocking her straight away to help her fall asleep again. It rather saddened me to see her that way.

Then one afternoon, towards the end of the day, she woke up and I happened to be sitting close to where she stood in her seat. I pulled her over and talked to her, touched her and sang to her. After a while she started to relax and eventually even to smile. She smiled at me for about twenty minutes or so, while we interacted. As we sat there facing each other, it suddenly hit me. Because small babies have no direct memory nor the ability to look beyond the present, when they are in pain, the world is pain, existence is pain and there is no hope or expectation of it ending. On the other hand, when they are happy the world is joy, life is joy, with no expectation of it ending.

So even if there is very little you can do for a child. If you can make it feel happy and loved for any amount of time, then for that amount of time, you have given the child a happy life. A life where happiness has no end. The realisation brought tears to my eyes at the time. This is only the first of many things Lili taught me. You will hear of her again.

I spent those first seven weeks in EAST trying to take in as much as possible of everything that went on. Most of my time was spent playing with babies, giving bottles. Changing nappies was not easy to achieve, since someone would invariably jump up and take over. Not because they did not trust me to do it properly, but because they seemed to feel I should be spared these 'nasty' tasks, even if I did not mind at all. If fact, I always felt a kind of triumph whenever I managed to escape notice and finish the entire routine of changing without getting 'caught'. This was very rare.

Aside from this, I went along with a foster care coordinator to visit some of the children in foster care near EAST. I went along one evening to pick up a baby from the train who had arrived from WEST with an *ayi* and an oxygen bottle. I went along to hospital, when that baby needed to have IV antibiotics. I wanted to experience every angle of the care provided.

While I had a lot of experience taking care of children, having worked as a nanny for several years and a babysitter before that, I had no medical knowledge at all. However I wanted to be of as much help as possible. So whenever an opportunity arose for me to add new skills to my repertoire, I would jump at the chance. I always went along on the medical rounds, which were also a good opportunity to find out who was who and what condition they had. I learned through hands on experience how to deal with seizing babies, babies on oxygen or fed through feeding tubes, nebulizing babies, etc.

Once I was there just over a month, I joined the children's home director when she was learning to place feeding tubes. Once we were both able to do this and had placed a few under supervision, one afternoon we went around all four apartments to pull out all feeding tubes that had been used for several weeks, taking turns in placing new ones. A practice run, you might say.

In the meantime Chinese Lunar New Year – now mostly called the Spring Festival – had arrived. This was celebrated with colleagues eating tremendous amounts of the traditional New Year's dish *jaozi*, dumplings with all kind of different fillings. And of course enormous amounts of fireworks. These had been going off for a month or more already, setting off car alarms all over the place. But when actual New Year's Eve arrived, all of that turned to nothing by comparison. The level of noise and smoke only allowed for a short time watching it up close. It was magnificent nonetheless. The year of the Pig had begun.

This was when I learned that New Year in China is not a one-day thing. It lasts for two weeks. From the New Moon to the Full Moon, when the Lantern Festival is celebrated to close off the New Year's celebrations. With, of course, more fireworks.

The Spring Festival is a family occasion, for which most people take a week to 10 days off. For some people, at the lowest levels of the work force, these might be the only days off they get in a whole year. The whole country is in motion, with migrant workers having to make their way home for the festivities. In the week – to two weeks – around New Year, it is utterly impossible to get tickets for any kind of public transport. Everything is sold out.

This means that the constantly revolving wheels of the foundation's children's homes grind to a halt. Children cannot be transported, so if there are particularly weak children in the outlying children's homes, they have to be dealt with on the spot. Hospitals discharge anyone who is not in immediate danger of dying by doing so, and will not admit any new patients – this last part already starts up to two weeks before New Year. Finally it is almost impossible to place children in new foster families around this time. This is because the foundation does not permit foster families to travel with the children. So if they have a foster child, they cannot go and visit other family members in different parts of the country. This is something most families make no problems about for the future, but this year….

All of this combined means that for two to three weeks, around Chinese New Year all the children's homes are stuffed to or beyond capacity and nothing at all is moving. Which for me, of course, was a perfect opportunity to finally get ahead in getting to know all the children in EAST.

Just before Chinese New Year, it was decided that I would be going to WEST to be the long-term resident foreign volunteer there. After EAST this is the biggest facility, with a relatively higher number of cases needing care, which veered more towards the medical. While as I mentioned I do not have a medical background, it was felt that I was learning relatively fast, so that I might be of use there. I would be going after Chinese New Year, but before the Lantern Festival, as soon as things started to move again and tickets for transport became obtainable. So on 1 March I got on the train to WEST, together with a member of the management staff and two babies. The first of many, many times that I would be travelling across China by train, caring for babies during the journey. On my way to my new home.

My introduction to WEST was a bit chaotic, because my arrival coincided with the three-monthly rotation of children's home directors. This would take place a day and a half after my arrival. It meant that the current director was up to her neck in getting everything organised and arranged for the upcoming hand-over. She had better things to do than to occupy herself with the rather bewildered new volunteer with whom she would in any case not be working together – for now –, since she was on her way out.

So the day after my arrival – which was late at night – I sat around waiting quite a lot, not too sure what to do. I was told I could just rest, but I wanted to get to know this new place. In the end I asked to be shown to the children's homes, so that I could occupy myself. Which I did. That Friday and Saturday I sometimes hung around in the office, to see if there was anything they wanted of me, and sometimes I would hang around in one or other of the children's homes, playing with the babies and getting to know things.

On Saturday the 'old' director left and the new one – she really was new, it was her first time as children's home director, although she had worked for the foundation longer – was in charge. This did nothing to make things less chaotic. Since she obviously needed a few days to figure out how everything worked and how to handle them. She also had better things to do than to explain to the new volunteer all the things she was still working to find out herself about this place. I was sympathetic with this. In time this director, Jian, became a good friend of mine and we figured out a lot of things together. The fact that she had some, but not very much English, was also great. She taught me a lot of Chinese.

Since structure was not forthcoming, I decided on Sunday to indeed take a day off. It had been a few weeks since I last did not spend time with the children at all for a full day. I spent the day reading, writing and exploring the neighbourhood a little, despite the rain. The rain was fantastic, by the way. It felt like there finally was 'weather'. At EAST the weather was always the same, blue skies, with the only varying degree of smog on any given day. Having lived all my life in countries where the weather is extremely changeable, I missed 'weather'. To me what we had at EAST was not weather, it was more like a background, a décor.

I felt refreshed and recharged after my day off. When on Monday it was clear that unless I do something, nothing would happen, I took things into my own hands and started my new routine. Not a very new one, basically it was the same as what I had done in EAST. I spent the morning in one group and the afternoon in the other.

WEST has two groups, which are more clearly divided than those in EAST. One apartment houses the toddlers, usually anyone who starts moving – crawling – is moved there. So the age range is roughly between 8 months and 3 years old. Normally there are about 10 toddlers here. Unlike the toddler group in EAST – EAST3 – the one in WEST has a structured daily routine. Breakfast at 7.00, fruit snack at about 9.00, lunch at 11.30 and after that a nap, another fruit snack at 15.00, dinner at 17.30 and by 20.00 most toddlers would be asleep. This is not strictly regimented. Smaller children, or children with special needs, who need more naps, and bottles etc. get them when required. But generally speaking there is a kind of structure to these children's lives, which is hard to provide in EAST3 because there children come and go too much, and a lot of them have just returned from hospital, which means they have their private regime.

In the other apartment, across the hall from the toddlers, are the WEST babies. Here like in almost all other places in the system, every baby has its own routine, or not. There are usually 13 to 17 babies cared for at any one time here. Their ages ranging from a couple of days to about one year old. If a baby is lagging behind in development – so does not start to move yet – it is often kept longer in the baby home. Either because their care is particularly complicated, or quite simply because of issues with space. It is often harder to add an extra baby to the toddler home, than to the baby home, because of the division of staff.

The set up of WEST was very simple. We had all three ground floor apartments of a regular apartment complex. Two of these were the children's homes, and one was our office/storage/kitchen. In the kitchen the *ayi* all had their lunch or dinner, which they brought from home, on their break. And there was one *ayi* who was there to cook for the children and for management. At lunch we would be called in to eat. The children's home director, the foster care director, the foster care coordinator, the two shift supervisors, the care supervisor, the cook and myself would share the meal. The cook in WEST was very good and I very much enjoyed her food – which was normal middle class home cooking – although in this area food tended to be somewhat spicier than I was used to. That needed a little more practice. For the first few months of my stay at WEST we also had an apartment on the fourth floor, which was the female – management – dorm. The one male member of our staff, the foster care coordinator, slept in one of the bedrooms in the office apartment.

I spent the next few weeks getting to know the children and the staff. Which was a little easier to do than at EAST because of smaller numbers and a lower instance of change. I got to know the American doctors who volunteered and came to check up on our children every Tuesday morning. These rounds continued to teach me more and more about medical care for the children, as did daily life. I saw the first babies being received straight from the *fuliyuan*, and was quite shocked at the state of them. Though I was to learn in time that the first two were not particularly bad off, they were about average cases.

I also gained my Chinese name. At first I had started to try and have people use my own name, but Chinese are not very good at pronouncing subsequent consonants, this does not exist in Chinese. So however hard they tried, they were only getting their tongues in a twist. After a week at WEST I had been asked for my Chinese name many, many times. So eventually I proposed they give me one, at the first supervisor meeting I attended at WEST. A week later Jian did in fact provide me with my new name, which from then on was used by all children's home staff. Its meaning is 'a flower's heart' and I have been complimented on it a lot. I am very grateful to Jian for naming me and helping me integrate.

The first two months at WEST rolled by relatively quietly. They were interspersed with a trip to Beijing when I had to have my tourist visa changed to a business visa to cover the whole year. A visit to EAST, and a very short visit to NORTH, which I wanted to see very badly, to get an idea of how things were there. It was arranged that I could go, but things kept shifting and changing. So in the end I travelled on the night train from EAST to NORTH, with a baby – so sleep was in very short supply. Then I spent the day in NORTH, which at the time consisted of only one home with 16 babies. It was great to see some of the babies there, whom I had known in EAST. And also to see the director, Hua, with whom I had worked in EAST and who now had rotated to NORTH. It was also an opportunity to get to know the other long-term foreign volunteer, an American girl, who lived at NORTH. That evening the other volunteer, an *ayi* and I got on the train back to EAST, with a baby each.

The first part of the night 'my' baby slept very peacefully, but that was the part that I spent talking to the volunteer. The second part of the night, no sleep was granted. So having skipped two nights, with no sleep in between, I was so tired I was dizzy, by the time we reached EAST in the morning.

A couple of times I got a cold and was very frustrated because I felt well enough to work, but could not go near the children for fear of infecting them. My cold could easily become their pneumonia. So each time I spent a few days in the office, trying to help out as best I could there, but having little to do. Apart from those little interludes, life was relatively uneventful at WEST. I worked five and a half days a week, taking Saturday afternoon and Sunday off.

While I enjoyed spending time with the babies, and was able to do little things – such as trying to get a two year old with dysphagia to overcome his oral aversion for everything except a bottle – I was increasingly feeling frustrated. By mid-April I felt did not want to go on anymore if this was the way it was going to be. My problem was that I wanted to really DO something. Feel that I was actually contributing something to the workings of the system, to the lives of the children, or the staff.

The way things were, of course it was good for children to get a little bit more attention, and it was pleasant for the *ayi* to have some of the pressure removed by my picking up a crying baby while they were feeding another. But essentially, I felt, if I would not show up, things would keep running just as well. In fact, if I would not show up, it would probably take quite some time for it to be discovered, because everyone would presume I was in the other home.

Before coming to WEST I had not received any clear idea of exactly what they wanted me to do here. Except that I was to write daily reports about the goings on. This issue became more and more important to me. I felt like a fraud, probably causing more trouble than being of help, while getting free room and board, and having been awarded a stipend as well. At Easter I sent an email to voice my doubts and frustrations to the CEO at EAST. I knew he was overrun with emails every single day and that it would probably be a long time before I would hear back, if at all, but I still wanted to get it off my chest.

A few days after this, I suddenly became extremely tired and I had a throat ache. I was afraid it might be mononucleosis, which would effectively have had me out for weeks if not months. After a few days the tiredness faded away, however, and the throat ache became worse and worse. On Tuesday I had the volunteer American doctor take a look and I was diagnosed with Strep Throat. I was put on penicillin, which did not help, the pain continued to increase, then I changed to a different antibiotic, which did help.

Once the pain was all gone and the doctor had confirmed I was no longer contagious, I was finally able to go back to the children, after having had to stay away for a week and a half. I could not wait. In my absence another baby had arrived from the *fuliyuan*, whom I had never met yet. On Wednesday 2 May I reappeared in the children's homes. And with that everything changed. I am still not sure exactly why or how things were suddenly different. But from that moment I was busy, needed and I never looked back.

It must have been something in my attitude, which changed. Improvement of my Chinese must also have played a role. However there seems to have been some kind of secret ingredient, which I never found out. Not that I mind, this is where my experience became truly worthwhile and rewarding.

Before I continue with my experiences in WEST, however, I am going to spin out a thread, which needs to be woven into the story from 1 February. While I started out volunteering for one organisation, it quickly became two.

The Hospice

Everything that happens in any of the children's homes of the foundation and everything connected to it, runs entirely on donations. Every cent, every piece of clothing and every item has been donated by someone. Like any other business, a charitable 'business' needs to 'sell' something to get money. What charitable organisations sell, is the feeling that you have made a difference in someone's life. Just like with any other business you have a certain market and you cannot just sell anything to these particular people. This can sometimes cause dilemmas.

What the foundation 'sells' is 'with the money you give, this child who is severely handicapped – or possibly in danger of losing its life – can receive the care it needs to live a – more – normal life'. By providing babies with the care they need and then move them into foster families, it is possible to keep a circulation going, bring in new children, who are helped etc. This way, at the end of the year, you can tell your sponsors: 'You have helped change/save the lives of this many children!' This makes people feel very good about themselves – and rightly so, without their sponsorship, it would not have been possible – and possibly inclined to give more.

By and large, this works wonderfully. However… in the care system there are two groups of children who cause a obstruction in the flow of the stream. One group is that of children with very complicated special care needs, who may live a long life, but cannot be put into foster care, because the risks are too high. The other group is that of terminal children. Children in this group have a medical condition, which cannot be remedied; they will not live to grow up. However this does not necessarily mean they are actually currently dying. They may well live for many months or possibly even years.

Beds taken up by both these groups are not free to be used by babies who would flow through and be followed by other children. Money used for the daily upkeep of these children cannot go to medical procedures of others. It is much harder to sell 'your money has paid for the upkeep of this baby in the last four month of its life' than 'you saved this baby's life'. Certainly you need a different target group to sell it to.

So one of the solutions proposed by the board in the USA, was to return terminal babies to the orphanages, seeing as they would die anyway. That way new babies could be accepted and helped. However everyone who works with the babies, in China, and who knows something about the conditions in the *fuliyuan* is squarely opposed to such an option.

The solution found for these babies is a hospice, outside of the foundation. Some people, who used to work for the foundation, left it and another foundation they had been involved in before joining this one, was revived. This revived foundation works on a Catholic premise and it managed to gather enough private funding to open a hospice. This home was opened in the same compound as EAST and took in babies not only from our foundation, but also from other foreign run children's homes in China and eventually even straight from certain *fuliyuan*. Starting with six babies, while the staff was still being recruited and trained, it had a capacity of ten – and has since moved and expanded.

From the very start I was involved with the hospice. I had gotten to know the director very well, through her links with the foundation I worked for. Of course I also knew all six babies who moved into the hospice on 1 February. I was there when they moved into their new home, a very momentous occasion.

The babies staying at the hospice have complicated heart defects, hydrocephalus at a stage too far advanced, or after failed shunt operations, severe liver conditions and severe seizure disorders, for the most part.

From the opening onwards, I spent some time in the hospice every single day whenever I stayed at EAST. In the weeks before leaving for WEST, I helped guide the still very inexperienced staff. Spending a lot of time with the most 'complicated' children, such as seeing the little boy who had a severe seizure disorder through his seizures, and getting the little girl with seven heart defects, who was nevertheless very strong-willed to sleep.

I even acted as shift supervisor for half a day, to help fill a gap in the roster when staff was scarce. This was a very valuable experience, because it showed me that working as a supervisor rather than a carer is a difference, which goes much further than just the actions you perform. I found that as a supervisor I was suddenly much further removed from the immediate contact with the children, and much more focussed on the care they needed instead. Keeping the overview all the time seemed to require taking a step back.

Having experienced this, I felt I definitely preferred the lower level of work. Not because I feared the responsibilities, but because I preferred to feel more connected with the babies. This is something, which I think did have an effect on me later on. While I ended up effectively being placed above the shift supervisors, I always retained a place between the shift supervisor and the *ayi* with regards to the closeness to the babies.

At the hospice, as at the children's home, there was a huge difference between what you would expect and what the situation was actually like. It sounds extremely sad and depressing, a home for children whom you know will never grow up. But it was not, not in the least. When you go to a hospice for adults, you enter a place where people are waiting for death, with or without fear. Babies do not wait for death. They do not know, nor care whether or not they have a future. They live in the now and at this moment they are alive: playing, laughing, throwing tantrums, taking their first steps, and generally enjoying life. This was something, which was apparent from the moment you set foot in the apartment.

Because it is known that the babies will die, when the time comes, they are lovingly surrounded by people who are sad to see them go, but accepting of the fact. They are made as comfortable as possible and held all the time – if they want to, some babies prefer not to be held towards the end – surrounded by support and love. That was really amazing to experience, and wonderful to be a part of.

I was amazed to find how I dealt with death in any case, in China. Whether it was at the hospice or in one of the children's homes. I had never been this close to death before, had never witnessed anyone dying. Now it was part of life. People said to me 'it must be very hard', and 'are you getting used to it?' But it was never a case of hard or getting used to it or not, for me. While it was always sad when a baby did not make it, I somehow could accept it. It was not something I set my mind to, or learned. It was an attitude I discovered I had.

In most cases I would have a good cry after a baby died, and would be quietly preoccupied with memories about them for a day or two afterward. That was the way it worked for me. What I felt very strongly was not a sense of failure at not having saved a baby. I felt that we still gave the baby something, even if it did not survive. By having been in our care, the baby had a fighting chance, and it died surrounded by loving care. Those are two very meaningful things. And while babies *have* died in my arms, I have sat with many more babies, whom I was certain did not have more than a couple of hours left to live, yet who are still alive today.

Getting Into It

When I returned to the children's home after my Strep throat break, I finally met Huang, a little boy with a cleft lip and palate, who had been received a week before at a few days old. The whole week he had doing relatively well. But now he had diarrhoea and he was starting to get progressively weaker. He was not drinking very well anymore and he was starting to show signs of dehydration.

    A few weeks previous we had lost a baby to dehydration. At the time I had been very worried about him and asked for advice. I felt we should do something more, but I was not quite sure what and felt restrained by the idea of 'who was I to intervene', when I knew so little about these things. In the end we sent him to EAST where he passed away the day after arriving. I had learned a lot from that case. I had seen the different stages the baby passed through. After he passed away, I asked a few doctors what to do in a case like that. Now that another case came around, I had a better idea of what I was dealing with and was determined to do all that I could to prevent a repeat of what had happened to the last baby.

    So this time I stepped over my hesitation to seem presumptuous and took charge. We placed a feeding tube to make sure that enough liquids could be administered while his feeding was poor. We gave him ORS - oral rehydration solution - in between all of his feeds and kept a very close eye on him. He started improving towards the evening and the next morning his skin was not as dry as it had been the previous day.

    Towards the afternoon, however, he became weaker. His fontanel fell again, he became more and more lethargic. He would not close his eyes anymore at all, not even to blink. We increased the ORS and placed gauze drenched in sterile saline water over his eyes to prevent them getting damaged by drying out. Not long after Huang threw up.

This, despite all reservations about the hospital, was our cue to rush him there. If he was throwing up what we put into him, there was no way for us to keep him hydrated, let alone substitute the fluids he was losing. He needed IV fluids. He was admitted to hospital straight away, together with an *ayi* and after four days in hospital he was still very weak, but he had recovered from the dehydration. We took him out of hospital in the morning and at noon, I boarded a train, to bring him to EAST. Huang made a full recovery, and in the meantime he has had his lip repaired and is in foster care waiting to reach the right age to have his palate repair surgery.

This was the turning point. It also is an indication of how I learned things along the way. While I have an innate tendency in new situations to say 'who am I to step in here', and an ever greater tendency to avoid confrontation or conflict. I slowly discovered another side to myself, which even I had never been aware of. While on my own behalf I am unwilling to upset or inconvenience people, when it came to the well being, or even life or death of a child, I did not let anything stand in my way. I fought for them and did not care whose toes I stood on in the process.

The learning part of this, the acquiring of new skills, increased as well over time. In a situation where it was clear that a baby had nothing left to lose, if no one else was able or willing to take a decision or act, I would. Sometimes my decision would be based on things I had seen or done before, sometimes only on an educated guess or instinct. However the situation was always such that if nothing was done, all was lost anyway. By trying something out, a baby might have its chances improved slightly. And surprisingly often, they did improve and pull through.

Where dehydration is concerned. After that first baby dying of it, no baby has died of dehydration again, in any location I was present. This while with the diarrhoea, which many babies suffered from when arriving from the *fuliyuan*, dehydration occurred or threatened to occur quite regularly. In fact, after Huang, none of them were even taken to hospital; they did not reach the point where they needed to, although some did come close.

Over the month of May, bit-by-bit I more and more took control of the medical side of things in WEST. This was not something I was particularly aspiring to or that I worked to accomplish. It seemed to be happening naturally. Usually with other people estimating my 'medical expertise' much greater than I did. More and more often I became, one of, the first to be called if there was a problem with a child.

By natural evolution, it seemed, I was starting to work longer hours and generally worked a six-day week now. Sunday still for the most part being a day to myself.

In the middle of May we had an American paediatrician visiting for a few days, she was volunteering and doing the rounds of all the locations. She spent a day checking up on the babies we had in the children's homes at WEST. Then she went to the outlying foster care programme we had in the same province about three hours south of WEST.

I asked permission to go along with her, from management in EAST. I wanted this both because I had never had an opportunity to visit this location and because spending two days with a paediatrician would be a fabulous learning opportunity. The reply I got was that they were about to ask me if I would be willing to go along with her, for those same reasons, and also to help her out if needed. So that was perfect.

This too was an amazing, albeit hectic experience. At the time there were almost 50 children in foster care in this village and the objective was to have them all seen, in two days. Because it is a rather remote rural location, they needed someone to look at the basic health of all the children and give advice more than any of the other locations. The way this was organised was that as much as possible foster families living relatively near to each other were asked to gather at one family's home. This way we did not need to spend quite as much time travelling.

It was wonderful to see all of these children, even though in some cases I was not entirely happy with the conditions. I did in fact learn a great deal from the paediatrician, who actively involved me and taught me things. Something for which I am incredibly grateful. By some miracle we managed to see almost every child, before getting on the bus back to WEST at 4pm the second day.

The final week of May was going to be a hectic one. Three months had passed, so it was time for the children's home directors to rotate, and on top of that it had been decided that in order to cut costs, the fourth floor dorm apartment would be given up and the office apartment would be changed into an office/dorm. All of this was quite enough to keep us busy, on top of the normal daily care for the children. But it was only the beginning, it all came to a head on the last Tuesday in May.

We thought it was just going to be an incredibly busy day. Both children's home directors were present for the handover, which would officially take place the next day. Tuesday was the day the volunteer doctor came to check on the babies in the morning. Plus it had been decided that the final move of all the stuff from the fourth floor apartment would take place that day, while the two directors were there to work together on it all.

This was only the beginning and background to what the day became however. Although the move was a major project, most of it passed me by, faded by what happened. Up to the arrival of the doctor at about 9.00, I helped with the moving, after that…

In the morning we got a phone call from a catholic mission that had received a newborn baby boy, with a hole in his abdominal wall and some of his intestines sticking out. They asked if we could accept him. Normally we would not have, because of the issue with the *hukou*, but this baby was in such a delicate state, that he would not survive if he did not have surgery straight away. So we conferred with central management in EAST and got permission to accept him. We would immediately put him on a train to EAST and on the other side, they would take him straight to hospital, to have his surgery. That was the plan. Then later on we would see if we could make some arrangement with a *fuliyuan* to get the baby a *hukou*.

The baby arrived in the middle of the doctor's rounds and it was instantly clear that he was very young, probably not yet a day old. He did not have a name, and he was in very bad shape. His oxygen saturation was low and his temperature was below 32°C – it did not register on an electronic thermometer. We put him on oxygen and wrapped up his intestines to prevent them from drying out. Because he was so extremely cold, I felt that warming him up with hot water bottles and covers was much too slow. So I volunteered to warm him up with body heat.

Since the baby needed to be on oxygen, the only place I had to lie down on was one of the baby beds, with my legs pulled up. We put the naked baby on my bare belly and covered both of us with hot water bottles and quilts. Because he was so very cold, we decided there was no way he could go to EAST. He might not make it to the station, let alone through an eight-hour train journey. So the *ayi* who had been arranged to accompany him on the train was sent home again and we hoped for the best.

Despite everything it was a funny experience, lying on a baby's bed, surrounded by people checking up on us and watching us closely. After a while I asked for a quilt to be wrapped around my legs. In response to questioning looks – it was about 30°C outside – I explained that it was not because I was cold, but because if I overheated, I would give off more body warmth. The newly arrived children's home director, Hua, got another quilt and tucked it around my drawn up legs. I had to laugh at the situation. I remarked that all I needed now was a pacifier. This set the others off laughing as well. But it only became really hilarious when a moment later the shift supervisor walked back in with a pacifier and seriously wanted to hand it to me.

After about an hour, the baby's temperature had been raised to 35.8°, nearing normal. There was a quick discussion and we decided to try and get him to EAST anyway. If he was to have any chance of survival at all, he needed surgery very soon. We needed to be quick though, the train would be leaving in just over an hour and we still had to get to the station and arrange tickets before that. The *ayi,* who would have taken him, had already gone and there was no time to make other arrangements. So I volunteered.

The baby was taken off my stomach and I had five minutes to get my stuff together and dress properly again, while they dressed the baby. The baby's bag was still packed and waiting for him. Our car had also left, since we had decided earlier that we would not need it. So Jian, the care supervisor and I almost ran to the taxis waiting at the entrance of the compound and urged the driver to get to the station quickly.

On the way the baby, whom I was holding, started throwing up yellow liquid and his breathing became more and more shallow. We were about ten minutes removed from the train station when I could not feel any breathing or heart rate anymore. Again, being in a taxi, I could not really say anything. So I simply stated that we needed to go back. The care supervisor looked at me and the baby and understood. She explained to the driver that the baby was throwing up and that we needed to go back, which we did.

A little while later he started throwing up and breathing again. However after that, there was no way we could put him on a train for eight hours. If a baby would die on a train, the potential consequences were disastrous. We always needed to weigh off the chances of survival and the need to be transported.

When we arrived at WEST the baby was still alive, but very weak. Attempts to place a feeding tube to deflate the swollen intestines failed. The baby continued to throw up yellow liquid and to breath weakly. An *ayi* from the toddler home, who is a nun – in WEST several members of staff are catholic sisters – was called and she baptised the baby Rou Wang. By now it was one o'clock or later, already past lunchtime. So the pressing need to eat resurfaced. For once, I flat out refused. It was very clear that Rou Wang had very little time left and I did not wanted him handed from one person to the next, just because I might get a little hungry if I stayed sitting there. I had to put up a big fight. One after another people came and said someone could take over from me, I should eat something first, etcetera, etcetera. But I held out and stayed there with him, while others had lunch – something that I did not begrudge them at all, there was no point in all of us hovering over him.

At two o'clock, just after the care supervisor returned from lunch, Rou Wang passed away. The first baby to die in my arms. The care supervisor and I cleaned him up, dressed him in clean clothes and wrapped him up in a thin blanket. We placed him in a cardboard box. Because of all the chaos of the move going on in the office, I put that box on what from that night onward would be my bed, out of the way. I took up position in front of the door, to prevent anyone wandering into the room and handling the box. Being badgered again, I agreed to having a bowl of food, and stood eating it, in front of the door.

Because this baby did not come from a *fuliyuan* and was a 'black baby', there were no formalities to go through after his death. He had officially simply never existed. Later on in the afternoon, when the car came back, the care supervisor and I brought Rou Wang back to the catholic mission where he had come from that morning. There a hole was dug for him, on a piece of ground beyond the vineyard, and he was buried in the box for baby formula, with the priest, the care supervisor, the driver and I attending.

Two totally unrelated things, which in my mind will always stay connected with the burial of Rou Wang, were for the first time in my life seeing a real scorpion in the wild, scurrying around. And seeing ants the size of baby mice. These were walking around while the priest was digging the hole. The ride home was quiet and bumpy.

The day after, the two directors did the hand over. Jian, together with whom I had learned so much about so many things, left for EAST, to take over there. It was sad to see her go. Although there was the consolation that at least she was going to EAST, where I made an appearance at least once a month, as opposed to NORTH where I had only set foot once in all my time in China.

Hua, who was taking over WEST was also a good friend, the one who had run EAST when I first arrived there. At this point she was more than seven months pregnant. She would only stay at WEST for a month, before going on maternity leave. Originally she would have stayed in NORTH for an extra month. However there were problems with staff who had been dismissed for unacceptable behaviour and who kept returning, using threats and even violence. Obviously no one wanted to leave a heavily pregnant woman exposed to a situation like that. For her another advantage to being in WEST, was that the WEST foster care director was her husband. In China it is not uncommon for husband and wife to be separated most of the time, because of work. But that does not mean they would not rather be together.

Being heavily pregnant did not mean Hua did not work very hard. However out of practical consideration, she told me that since she would only be there a month and I was a constant presence at WEST, and because I was already taking over more and more of the medical care of the children's homes as it was, she would leave it to me and the care supervisor to basically take care of that side of things. Of course we discussed everything and for major decisions we needed her permission and she needed to be the one to communicate with EAST if their permission was needed. But on the whole she would go with our recommendations and if urgent action needed to be taken, we could go ahead and do so without consulting her.

Hua and her husband had an apartment in the city, so if there were no major problems – and she always asked me if it was all right with me – she would go home at the end of the day on Saturday and return on Sunday evening or Monday morning. Leaving me in charge. Since Sunday was the only day the care supervisor had off, I really was the only person in charge on those days. Although I could always call both the director and the care supervisor and either or both would have come immediately if there were serious problems. And so the seven-day week was born. It would last to the end of my stay in China. I usually did try to get a few hours to myself on Sunday. But whether I could actually get them, depended on what was going on.

Thus ended the month, which shot me from feeling rather useless and superfluous to being suddenly an essential little wheel in the workings of the system. By this time the feelings of deep dissatisfaction, which I had experienced only a month ago, were not only gone, but also mostly forgotten. I headed forward, without a backward glance.

Forming a Perfect Unit

That is really what we were and became more and more. Two parts forming a perfect unit. The way I would explain it to people is, that we were like Batman and Robin. The difference between us and most of those kinds of duos was that we would both, honestly and sincerely, claim that we were Robin. Which is probably part of why it worked so well.

The person I am talking about is the care supervisor at WEST. I will call her Sun. She has worked at WEST from the moment it was set up in 2004 and she has made herself completely indispensable. That is not just my opinion, but the general opinion of those working for the foundation in China. It is illustrated by the fact that she is now – and has been since November 2007 – the only care supervisor. In all other locations the position has been eliminated, but no one would think of getting rid of her. While on the other hand, even if they did eliminate the position altogether, she has assured me that would not chase her away at all. She would just continue to work as an *ayi*, even though that would mean almost halving her salary.

Sun is a warm, dedicated woman, completely devoted to the care of the children. If you call her at ten o'clock at night, or at five in the morning, she will be there in five minutes. I know, because it has happened. At uneventful times – which are rare – she works from eight to six, six days a week. However if there is anything that needs to be taken care of or needs to be monitored, she will stay as long as it takes and suggest herself to come in early.

The way she is able to work the system, is unrivalled. Always in a polite, friendly way, but getting it done. When transporting the children to EAST, a decision is often made last minute. Either because their condition suddenly worsens, or because we receive them in such bad shape, that they need to go to EAST straight away. Last minute it is extremely hard to get train tickets in

China. Especially since on an eight-hour journey with a sick baby, we prefer to travel on a hard sleeper rather than on a cramped chair in between two other people. Over time Sun has developed a network at the train station near WEST, which means that as long as she is with us, we can walk into the station without a ticket – officially impossible – and arrange a bed just before getting onto the train. This without her or any other person who comes along to help us onto the train even having to buy a platform ticket.

The same goes at the hospital. She manages to cut waiting times, get appointments and at times even bargain down the price of a test or procedure. All in aid of the 'poor abandoned babies'. At the hospital this is so hard to do, that, if at all possible, all is done to avoid a situation where she cannot accompany a baby who needs to see a doctor. To the point where if several things coincide, Sun will be sent to hospital and for instance the children's home director will do more 'menial' jobs.

However while this is all high praise – which does not begin to do her justice – competence does not guarantee a good working relationship. There has to be more than that, and there was. Somehow we seemed to be exactly on the same wavelength. We understood each other and complemented each other. In a way, which cannot be described, nor really understood – even by me – the two of us together really did seem to make up a new and better whole.

For instance, communication. When I first came to WEST, my Chinese was still very poor. While it improved relatively rapidly, there were always great gaps and lots of room for misunderstanding and miscommunication. Although I could only speak Chinese with Sun and my Chinese was very limited, we were on the whole able to communicate very well. She was even able to interpret for me. I would say something about the care of a child to her, in broken Chinese, and she would then explain it properly to other caregivers.

The times when I was really making a mess of it and she could not understand at all what I was on about – something which became rarer and rarer, probably more because of her learning to understand the kind of mistakes I made than because of my progress – she would not say anything, nor ask anything. She would simply get a look of infinite patience on her face, and I would know I was completely off track and needed to find another way of describing what I wanted to bring across. Eventually we would always make our way to understanding.

Sun has taught me a great deal, about a great many things. She is very intelligent and capable. Our real cooperation began in May, when I suddenly stepped up and started doing something. Quite soon I began to see that she was a lot like me, in that she very much wants to learn new things, in order to be better able to help the children. The difference between us is our background. I will simply go up to people and ask them to show or explain me things, so that I can understand them better. Being a Chinese middle class woman in her late forties, Sun would never presume to ask her 'superiors' – doctors, physiotherapists, specialists, foreigners, etc. – to disclose their 'trade secrets'. That is just not done.

Once I realised this – both her eagerness to learn and her reticence in gathering information – I actively involved her in all that I was learning, as I went along. For instance at one point I decided I wanted to learn to use the stethoscope. We had one at WEST and it seemed to make sense to me to try and figure out how to use it so that in future I would be able to listen first and decide whether we needed to go to a doctor to get a problem confirmed. The way I went about this, was simply to pick up the stethoscope every time we had gotten a diagnosis and listen to the baby's lungs to see if I could pick up on the differences in sound between just phlegm in the lungs, asthma, bronchitis, tracheitis and pneumonia. Later on, I was also instructed by several doctors in distinguishing the different sounds.

So one time I was listening to a baby's lungs and Sun stood by watching me with interest and curiosity. When I asked her if she wanted to have a listen, she started by shaking her head with an embarrassed giggle, but then after a second's thought, she nodded her head eagerly. Over time we both became quite proficient at pre-diagnosing babies by listening to their lungs. And it went the same way with the otoscope – the devise for looking into ears. However I could never convince her of our equal capability. If I was around, she would always ask me to listen first. Thankfully however, she was not afraid to tell me if she did not agree with me. On the occasions when she did question my conclusion, she was usually right.

I have never seen information or knowledge as a commodity to be hoarded and then used as a weapon against others, or to build a pedestal out of, from which to look down on others. I will be the first to admit that I am extremely greedy for knowledge and I love gathering it. But for me learning something and passing it on to others is something that happens almost in a single motion. To me it seems like the only logical thing to do. I truly enjoy explaining thing to people who are interested to find out about them. Thankfully we both worked that way.

Apart from passing on as much as possible all information that I gathered along the way – the part of it which did not come from her to begin with, of course – I also mentioned her eagerness to learn to the American doctors who visited us. They were more than happy to point out things to her; it was just that they were used to be asked.

Something else, which I admire very much in Sun, is her open mindedness. A lot of people in their late forties, Chinese or otherwise, have become relatively set in their way of thinking. Especially when big, medical things are concerned. With Sun I found that if you explained something to her, which was contrary to what she had always known to be true, she would weigh it seriously and often adjust her opinion.

Big examples are for instance that in China traditionally a mother and baby are not to leave the house at all in the first month after the baby is born. It is considered detrimental to their health to do so. So when we had a relatively severely jaundiced baby of a few days old, and I suggested taking it outside for a while to expose it to direct daylight – the weather being very nice – this was received by everyone with shock and horror. I received permission to do it anyway, from an American who was at the top of the medical decisions chain, so they let me go out, though horrified. Sun noticed that the jaundice did actually recede relatively quickly, with the trips outside. And when the next jaundiced baby arrived, she did not bat an eyelid when I announced I would take it out. While others still laughed. The time after that, she suggested it herself.

An even bigger one was the vaccinations. In China doctors say that children with mental handicaps cannot be vaccinated. This supposedly is a danger to their brain. Sun had asked them, but obviously decided against having the mentally handicapped children vaccinated after hearing that, from 'the experts'. During the summer we were confronted with measles and it was when we were going over the immunisation records that I found out we had several children who had not been vaccinated, and was told the reason. I told Sun that in Europe and America children are vaccinated regardless of their mental capabilities and that this does not cause any problems. She did not need to give it a second thought. She immediately said that next time we would not say or ask anything to the doctor, we would just say 'this baby is next'. And that is exactly what happened. All the babies at WEST got vaccinated.

Sun was a great support to me as well, especially after Hua was replaced by a director with whom I did not get on very well. Without Sun, I do not know how I would have gotten through those months. In all my adult life, I do not think I have ever trusted anyone as completely and unconditionally as I do Sun. Both with my own life and with that of the babies. And that is saying a lot.

Trails and Triumphs

At the start of June I went to EAST and spent a few days there. There were several reasons for this. I was to have a few meetings with management people, a kind of evaluation of how things were going, now that I had found my place in the workings of things. I also went to pick up two babies, who would form the start of a new project, which I will get into in a moment. And finally, unknown to me, the CEO wanted to make a proposal.

With the hospice up and running four months now, attention was turned to the other category of children who 'clog up the system': the unfosterable children. I was offered the opportunity to help set up and then run a long term care facility which would take in these children and care for them indefinitely, freeing up the beds in the children's homes.

I was tremendously flattered by this offer. In a certain way, the idea did appeal to me. I knew that I would be very good at something like that and that I would enjoy it. I had in fact already given this some thought beforehand, even though I never expected to ever be offered something like this. My involvement with the hospice had made me consider what it would be like to do something like that. One of the conclusions I had already come to, before an offer was ever made, was that while on one hand, I would be an especially suitable candidate for a job like that. On the other hand, I would be singularly unsuitable.

I knew myself well enough to know that if I would ever do something like that, I would not be able to do it at less than a hundred percent. Meaning that I would be unlikely to ever allow myself an hour, let alone a day or more, off, to just spend on myself – or who knows go and visit family back in Europe, once in a while. I knew that there would always be something going on with the children and that I would always put their needs before mine. I was fully aware that when you live like that, in the end you will run yourself into the ground.

All of this I was aware of. While at the same time, I had no idea. At the time I was getting more and more involved in the work I was doing, but I had not by a long shot reached the point I envisaged myself in should I take on the running of a care facility. It would not be long before I would find out exactly what that entailed, though under different circumstances.

So while I was very flattered with the trust they showed in me, I turned down the offer. For the reason mentioned above, and also for the one mentioned in the introduction, namely that I did not feel I wanted to live in China for several years. Setting up a long-term care facility would need a commitment of at least four or five years. They were very understanding and there were no hard feelings, although there was some disappointment.

However, while I had turned down the running of the long-term care facility, the kind of work that I would have been doing there, soon found its way to me anyway. I had no objections to that. When I returned to WEST, I brought two babies with me – travelling with an *ayi* of course, on the train care is always one to one – who normally would not have left EAST. Both of them were long-term feeding tube dependent. Something, which usually meant that they would stay in EAST because of complicated special needs and to be monitored. The head of the medical department, however, had asked me if I would be willing to work with them, to see if I could get them off their feeding tubes. The reason she asked me was that I had been working with babies with feeding difficulties in previous months, booking very small successes. In EAST they had tried everything they could think of, so there was not much to lose if I would not succeed, it was a question of grabbing at last straws. I was happy to give it a try. Since I lived in WEST, that is were the babies came to.

One of the babies I will call Yan. He was a five-month-old boy with spastic cerebral palsy; mentally he was alert. I knew him when he was a newborn, having just arrived in EAST – a week or two after I got there. When he came in he had a big 'water balloon' on his head, which disappeared on its own very rapidly.

One of the things which I will never forget about the time I spent with Yan, when he was that small, was that after having held him for about 5 to 10 minutes I shifted my fingers and found that my thumb had left an imprint on his head. An indentation, which disappeared very, very slowly. This was due to the swelling of his head and did not do any damage. But it left a huge impression on me. I had never left finger marks on a baby's head before.

The state of his head was a telling sign of a very difficult birth. It soon became apparent that there had been brain damage in the process of the birth. One of the big problems he had was that he had no swallowing reflex, so he had to be fed by feeding tube from the start.

While feeding tubes are great for getting food into babies who are unable to feed themselves, they should only be used short term. The human body does not like having foreign objects present and after a period of tolerance, it will usually start to reject them. Which can cause serious damage. In the western world people who are unable to eat by themselves for long periods will have a G-tube placed, which goes straight into the stomach through the abdominal wall, instead of being inserted through the nose and oesophagus into the stomach. Unfortunately this was not an option where we were.

The first few months of life, eating is something, which is driven by reflexes. Around about six months of age, it becomes a more deliberate action. The aim was to see if it would be possible to get Yan to actively eat, even though he had not had any previous eating experience.

Oddly enough it seemed like he was conscious of having a feeding tube, small as he was, and he did not like it. Every time he was fed through the tube – which was every two hours –, he kicked up a great fuss. This made feeding him a lot harder, because crying and coughing cause an upward pressure in the feeding tube, which is stronger than the gravity that usually lets the milk flow down. When a baby throws a tantrum, milk and air sometimes even come back up through the feeding tube.

Already on the train back to WEST I noticed that Yan was moving his mouth a lot, as if he did want to drink. So I tried giving him a little milk, by dropping it into his mouth with a syringe. To my astonishment and delight he swallowed. He only took about 10mls, but at least one thing was established, he was able to swallow. That meant that the biggest hurdle was overcome, even if many smaller ones were still waiting.

Arriving at WEST with two feeding tube dependent babies, my life suddenly got a lot busier. The carers at WEST were not used to dealing with long-term feeding tube dependency. Before, if a feeding tube was placed at WEST either the baby would gain strength and have the feeding tube removed within days – a small minority –, or they would be so weak that they would either not live very long, or be moved to EAST within a couple of days. So over the next couple of weeks I would regularly be called – day or night – to either explain that something was not a problem but simply a normal side effect of long-term feeding tube use, or to take care of a problem if there really was one.

While Yan's first step towards feeding – the swallowing – was easily taken, the road from then on was not in any way smooth. Every day I would try during as many feeds as possible to get him to take as much as possible by himself, trying all kinds of different methods of dropping and using different nipples. I could always get some of it into him, but before long he would get fed up and lose interest, throwing a tantrum if I persisted.

This went on for about a week and no progress was evident. So I decided to take it a step further. In advance I announced a day where no one was allowed to give Yan anything through his feeding tube. I wanted to see if hunger would motivate him. This can go two ways, it is possible for hunger to act as a motivator, but there is also a risk that a baby gets so upset with hunger that he or she will not cooperate anymore. Still it was worth a try. If Yan would really go ballistic, we could always use the tube to feed him after all. Besides I have found that letting a baby go hungry for a limited period, is not just a potential motivator for the child. It is an excellent motivator for the carer – including myself – who will go to much greater lengths to get food into the baby if they know that if it does not go through the mouth, it will not go in at all.

In Yan's case, it worked. Initially I was the only one allowed to feed him, every two hours I would sit down with him and try to get as much into him as possible. Starting with droppers and eventually moving on to bottles with nipples designed for babies with cleft palates – these require less effort to get the milk out of the bottle than regular nipples. He did not take quite as much as he was supposed to. But it was close enough not to worry about him being deprived, and intake improved.

The greatest challenge with Yan was not the technical, physical eating, but keeping him interested. He would get bored with it quite quickly and unless he was kept entertained, he refused to go on. Once we figured that out, I would feed him while walking around the apartment, letting him look at toys and people. Towards the end of a feed, when that did not suffice anymore, another person would stand beside me waving a toy in his face and talking to him. That proved to be effective.

Yan did really well that day. For the night staff, I did not leave special instructions, because I felt Yan should have the opportunity to rest after all of his hard work during the day. Still the next morning I heard that even during the night he had taken some of his feeds by mouth. I was really pleased with his progress, but not quite ready yet to remove the feeding tube. I wanted to see if he could keep it up for a few days first.

Yan had different ideas about that. After having done well a second day, this time being fed by *ayi* as well as myself and still improving his intake, he pulled out his own feeding tube that evening. No need for that anymore. As it happens, he was right. I decided to leave it out for the moment, as long as he was doing well and it was never placed back. While I provided the initial start, a lot of credit needs to go to the *ayi* who managed in quite a short time span to increase the volume of his intake so much that he could go to three hourly feeds instead of two hourly.

A couple of months later, Yan was introduced to his first solid food: fruit mash and vegetable mash. After about a week of getting used to the change, a time most babies need, he loved it and did well with that too. Since then his eating has developed much like that of his peers.

The other baby who came to WEST together with Yan, I will call Yur. She was almost nine months old at the time. She has a very severe seizure disorder. When she returned to WEST, despite – or so we thought at the time – being on two kinds of anti-convulsive medication, she had 30 to 40 seizures per day, about ten of which would last up to half an hour. While on the other hand the medication sedated her to the point where she was asleep literally all the time. Her life consisted solely of sleeping and seizing. What is more, she had lost all of her reflexes, as a result of the medication, including her swallowing reflex. This meant that she was completely feeding tube dependent.

Her neurologist was not willing to change anything about her medication. Since like this she had no quality of life whatsoever, I had been asked if I was willing to try and experiment with her medication, thereby hopefully reducing the number of seizures she had and increasing her awareness. Since Yur did not have anything to lose, I agreed to take on the challenge.

We used information from 'Disabled Village Children' by David Werner as a guideline and on the internet I read up on the medication she was on: Topamax and Depakine. The basic plan was to change her over from these to Phenobarbital. Although it was a risk, because she was already having so many seizures a day, some of which quite severe, I really wanted to try and wean her off the Topamax and Depakine first, before putting her on Phenobarbital. I wanted, if possible, to get a baseline, to see how much of the problems she had at that moment were a side effect of the medication, and how much was simply due to brain damage – either from the medication or from the seizures. I asked and got permission to do this. With the plan B always in place that if her seizures would increase in severity or frequency dangerous to Yur, we would immediately put her on Phenobarbital and continue to wean her off the other medication while giving her that.

Anti-convulsive medication is dangerous stuff. You cannot just stop using it, you need to decrease the dosage very gradually, otherwise dangerously severe seizures could be the result. So before starting to decrease her dosage, a lot of maths had to be done. I made a schedule with dates specifying which medication was to be reduced to how much, when. Until the Topamax 'ran out' I decreased the two in alternating steps: Topamax lowered, then four days later, Depakine lowered, then Topamax, etcetera.

To be able to keep track of how Yur was doing, I had the *ayi* keep a seizure log, starting two days before we started changing her medication. They recorded the time, duration and nature of the seizure – this last part I had broken down in nine features, coded by numbers, which they wrote down. This way I could do a daily count of the number of seizures and their severity.

Apart from the education needed about feeding tubes, for both Yan and Yur, I also had to train carers in dealing with seizure disorders. Especially at the start, I spent a great deal of time caring for Yur myself, holding her through her seizures. This was both because I was not yet confident that *ayi* were able to deal with it correctly – instinctive reactions such as trying to restrain her arms to make her stop moving, which can have potentially disastrous consequences, were common – and because a lot of the *ayi* were afraid when Yur had a bad seizure. They had not witnessed that kind of thing before.

Initially I would get glances of clear disapproval at the 'cold' way in which I dealt with the situation. Since we did not have diazepam available there was nothing we could do but hold Yur, making sure she had complete freedom of movement without fear of hurting herself and wait for the seizure to pass. I could sense the exasperation at the fact that I was doing nothing to make it stop. The only thing I would do was be there for her, and sometimes sing to her. There was one particular song, 'The Steps of St Paul's' from Mary Poppins, which I sang to her a lot.

This period is one of those, which underline the amazing teamwork between Sun and me. My complete trust in her, allowed me to spend the best part of most days by Yur's bedside – she shared a room with Yan, and later Lili, allowing me to look after the most complicated cases simultaneously. I knew that Sun was keeping an eye on the 26 other children we had in our care, and if there was a problem with one of them, she would come to me and we would look at it together. This provided me with the luxury of being able to focus completely on Yur – and at other times, other difficult cases – without a worry.

What happened over the weeks that we spent reducing Yur's medication was quite remarkable. Only just over a week after we started reducing her dosage, we noticed that suddenly she would make sucking motions with her mouth, in her sleep, from time to time. This gave us hope that she would one day be able to eat by herself again, as she had before she was put on anti-convulsives.

What amazed me even more than that, and it took me a long time to dare believe it – since it is known that any kind of change in anti-convulsive medication can bring about a change for the better or the worse which is very short lived – was that as she received lower dosages, her seizures became less in number. She did have one or two seizures every day, which were longer than the longest ones before, sometimes even up to 50 minutes. However the bulk of the seizures became shorter in duration and less in frequency and severity.

In less than a month, she started to wake up a little at times, not being always asleep, whenever she was not seizing. As soon as this started to happen, she drank! Her reflexes were returning and within a few days, she was drinking bottles as if she had never done otherwise. In fact, pretty soon we needed to slow her down, because she was drinking so fast that she would make herself sick. Downing 120-160ml in 5 minutes flat.

Waking up did not mean getting back being a normal nine month old. She would have her eyes open and move her head and arms around, but she was not directly responsive. Still it was an enormous improvement to her previous state. The first day she had enough awareness to cry because she felt discomfort – something that had not happened for months – I wanted to cry for joy. I was so moved by that sound.

Slowly Yur began to spend more and more of her time awake. Very, very slowly her awareness of her surroundings improved, leading her to cry more and more. It was not easy for her, suddenly being aware of her surroundings again. Having been shut off from the world for several months, being aware of sounds and movement and colours and everything at once, led to sensory overload. She would start to cry inconsolably, distraught by everything coming at her.

The problem was that there was very little we could do for her in these situations, because holding her, patting her, rocking her, all increased her sensory input. Eventually I resorted to holding her very, very still, while singing the song, which I had sung to her so often while she was still beyond reach. This usually helped her calm down after a while. It was something familiar.

While on the whole she was improving day by day, some time in July I made an unfortunate discovery. I realised that what we had taken for very mild seizures while she was awake, initially, was in fact athetoid cerebral palsy. This is a form of cerebral palsy where a person is unable to stop moving. If you hold all of their limbs restrained, they will move their head. Once I realised this, I observed Yur more carefully with this in mind and realised that while awake, she was in fact always in motion. Sometimes it seemed like she was completely calm and relaxed, but if you watched closely, you noticed that she was still making minute movements with her fingers and toes. This was something, which nothing can be done about; it will stay with her for life. It was probably caused by lack of oxygen in some part of the brain during a particularly bad seizure.

As her medication was further reduced, to my amazement so did the frequency of her seizures continue to decrease. To the point where when she was completely taken off all medication, she only had two or three seizures a day, which lasted less than ten minutes each. I was astonished that this was accomplished by only taking her off all medication. When I enquired in EAST exactly how her seizures had been when they decided to put her on medication, I learned that after she was put on Depakine, her seizures had in fact become more and more frequent. At the time it was thought that this was probably because her condition was deteriorating so fast that the Depakine was not sufficient to control the seizures. A neurologist who was consulted, added Topamax to give more control, but this did not have any effect, apart from sedating her. So it seems like it might have been the medication making things worse, rather than her own condition.

We kept her off all medication for two weeks before introducing the Phenobarbital. During that time, there were even seizure free days. Since she started on the Phenobarbital, on a low dose, she has not had any more seizures and she has not become any more sleepy. In fact the process of Yur increasing her awareness and consciousness continued over many, many months. This process took – or takes, as I am not entirely convinced that she has reached her full potential yet, now, seven month after being off Depakine completely – longer than the total time she had been on the medication which caused her to lose these faculties.

There is something else which I find remarkable. Something which could have just been a coincidence if it had only been Yur I had seen it with, but which I have seen in other babies I have since weaned off Depakine. That is that at or close to one year of age these babies on Depakine still did not have a single tooth. About a month after they were completely off the Depakine, their first tooth promptly arrived and others followed.

All in all, after all that I have seen connected with it, I have become a great opponent of giving Depakine to infants. While unfortunately it seems to be the drug of choice by those who prescribe it. And not just in China.

The work I did with the babies was physically and mentally demanding. Working long days, seven days a week, sometimes getting up several times during the night. Trying to take an hour's nap after lunch to catch up a little. Dealing with prolonged 'projects' like the two just described alongside the daily occurrences like pneumonias, unexplained fevers, unexplained spots. And in one case a baby who turned out to react quite violently to fever suppressing medication, causing her temperature to drop far too low for several hours, before it rocketed up again, leaving us no choice but to give her something to bring it down again – in increasingly lower doses – which went on for a week.

Still I did not feel this was particularly trying. Because while it did of course take a lot of energy, I got so much back at the same time. Not just satisfaction, also actual energy. It was almost like a self-perpetuating cycle of investing energy and receiving it back. The problems we faced with children, which sometimes seemed sheer insurmountable, did not appear as trials to me either, I viewed them more as challenges, which I was happy to do my best to meet.

This does not mean that there were no trials during my time in China of course. Only that they did not come from my work with the children. They came from a different corner: having to deal with incompetent people. This was a great trial for me. In WEST I was very lucky, because there were very few people who did not do their job well and with joy, and who were not willing to learn. There were a few, like you will find anywhere. In this I discovered a side of myself I was not familiar with. I found out that I was able to outright criticize people and without regard for their feelings put them in their place if I felt that their way of working was putting the well being of babies at risk and they did not respond to earlier friendly pointers for improvement. Over time I became less and less reticent in situations like these. I became aware that while people who were competent and/or willing to improve admired me, I was feared and disliked – to put it mildly – by those who were not.

The greatest trial came my way at the end of June, and was there to stay. The last week of June it was time for the Hua to be substituted so that she could go on maternity leave. The newly arriving children's home director was young and inexperienced. This was known ahead of time. Now that I already had a firm hand in the running of the children's homes, the idea was for me to help out and train the girl, whom I will call Hai, so that over time she would be able to look after things by herself more and more.

At the start, to me it seemed a challenge rather than a trail, and one that I welcomed. I looked forward to helping and teaching her. This positive attitude faded quite soon, however. The greatest problem I came across was what I perceived as her complete and utter lack of common sense. When I first got to know Hai, I was at times quite shocked at the completely ridiculous and irresponsible solutions she came up with and decisions she wanted to make. I did my best to explain to her, every time, why that might not be such a good idea and to present her with an alternative. Almost all the time my advice would be taken, and to start with I did not mind too much, because she was after all still learning. But it soon became apparent that she did not take that information and implement it the next time she came across a similar situation. In other words, there did not appear to be much learning going on.

After a while this began to really sap my energy, because I needed to keep an eye on her all the time to make sure no irreversible or dangerous decisions were taken in my absence. It also made me completely paranoid about what might be happening whenever I was not present.

Hai was afraid of medical responsibility. Something, which is not a plus in someone who is running a medical children's home. Of course I was there to take that responsibility. But while I expected her to learn and bit by bit get more involved, what actually happened was that she withdrew more and more. Not only leaving it all to me, but also not wanting to be told about it. I felt it was my duty to at least inform her of everything that was going on in *her* children's home, even if I took the medical decisions, but it regularly happened that she walked out of the room or changed the subject when I tried.

One evening I was sitting with a baby who was in such bad shape that it seemed almost certain that she only had a few more hours to live. Hai was called and I asked her if she was ready to lose her first baby. Her answer was a desperate 'NO'. Followed by the remark that this could not happen. I could not muster anything more in response to that than to say that she had better get ready soon then, and focussed on the baby again. The baby did in fact survive, not only that evening, but still. But Hai's reaction was telling.

Of all the things that annoyed me, and there were many, the thing that got to me most, was that she would provide EAST with incorrect information about children's conditions. In many cases she did not really understand the situation, even when it was explained to her. When she contacted EAST for advice – since she was the children's home director, these communications went through her – about a baby, she would nevertheless answer all the questions put to her. If she did not actually know or understand the answer, she would make one up. I could accept decisions not to bring babies to hospitals or EAST, as they were sometimes made for monetary reasons or because it was felt that the chance of really improving the baby's condition was too slight, but only as long as they were based on full knowledge of the actual situation.

On one occasion we were at the hospital with a severely jaundiced baby, the verdict was that she should be admitted to the intensive care unit. Before making big expenses like that, we always needed to contact EAST, where they had an overview of the money available and the priority of the cases in all the different locations and ask for their permission. So Hai made the phone call and I heard her tell the person on the other side that yes, the baby was a bit yellow, but she was eating, sleeping and pooping well. Personally if I had been the person on the other side, I would have thought, 'it is nice to know the baby is doing so well, but why are you calling me?'. Thankfully by now Hai's tendency to do this was known and they asked to speak to me. I gave a little more information and it was decided the baby was to come to EAST immediately. With only an hour to go until the train left, and only the two of us present, with the baby, we rushed to the train and I brought her to EAST. We had the baby's things, because we knew she might have to stay in hospital, I had nothing with me.

After three weeks of working together with Hai, I was at the end of my tether. I was physically and mentally completely exhausted. On the one hand wanting to stay as much out of her way and in the children's homes with the children and Sun to escape it all. On the other hand not daring to let her out of my sight. I wrote an email to EAST to let them know that the situation was unsustainable. The reply was that they understood, but that unfortunately there was no replacement for her, they were recruiting new directors, but had not succeeded yet, so there was not much they could do.

The person in charge of the children's home's and foster care directors came down to WEST and talked to Hai. She stayed around for a few days, allowing me to withdraw completely from all management responsibility and concentrate on the work with the babies. Which helped me recharge. She also told me not to take everything onto myself. That for them at EAST to really be able to see how Hai worked, they needed to see her make mistakes.

From that time on, I did not interfere with the logistics, admin or contact with the *fuliyuan* anymore, and only placed myself squarely between Hai and anything to do with the children's welfare. This did provide me with a little bit more breathing space. Still my patience with Hai continued to grow thinner and thinner. At a certain point I was so tired and frustrated with it all, that unfortunately I did not have a good thing to say about her anymore and treated her unfairly at times. I just did not have it in me to make anymore allowances.

Still it is not to be inferred that my life was a misery from then on, it just became a little more challenging. Most of my time was still spent with the babies and I continued learning and helping. At the end of July we had four American volunteers staying with us for a few days, three of whom were physiotherapists. They did great work with our children and taught Sun and me a lot of exercises for the children with different forms of cerebral palsy.

When we got into a daily routine of doing physiotherapy on each of these children, twice a day, I found it absolutely astounding how fast they progressed. One little boy, who was already a year old, but still unable to even hold his head up, learned to sit up by himself in the course of just over a month. That was really a sight to see. The first week or so he would scream every time we made him do his exercises, but slowly he started enjoying himself more and more, sitting upright and looking around him.

There was yet another big 'project' for me to lose myself in. Once Yan and Yur had both started to drink by themselves, no longer needing their feeding tubes, I was asked if I would consider trying again whether it would be possible to get Lili to eat and/or drink on her own. I had started working with her before I came to WEST and while I had accomplished something, unfortunately no progress had been made since I had left. Lili had been feeding tube dependent almost a year already. The tube was starting to cause real damage, internally. If we could not find a way to make her eat by herself, her prospects were not good at all.

    I happily accepted the challenge. I was delighted at the prospect of having Lili near again. I had a special connection with her and I missed her, now that I was away from EAST. It was a very unusual step though. Lili would be the first NORTH baby to come and stay at WEST in the history of the foundation. Children were regularly moved to EAST and back, but never between the outlying homes. The *fuliyuan* had better not find out about it either, as they were likely not to be pleased about it.

    I went to EAST to pick Lili up, and was very happy to be taking her away. Because she is an easy, quiet baby, whenever things get busy, she is the one who gets left to 'play' on her own. While because of the cerebral palsy she needs a lot of stimulation to activate her. So when I saw her in EAST2, she seemed lethargic and somewhat depressed. She just lay there with her head on the headrest. I was determined to draw her out of her shell.

    I did. The eating part was not at all straightforward. For a month I tried absolutely everything I could think of: six or seven different kinds of nipples, drinking from a sipping cup, drinking from an open cup, letting milk flow along my finger while she chewed it to a pulp, using a dropper or a syringe. Most times, the first time she would take as much as 10-15 mls, raising our hopes, just for a moment. After that it would go downhill fast, until she would refuse to take anything that way again. I even once, against my better judgement, tried to push through her resistance, to see if that would help – more because everyone seemed to think it would than because I did, plus everything else had been tried. She just got so upset that she would not let anything go near her mouth again for the time being.

By the end of this time, I was at the end of my wits. I was racking my brain trying to think of other methods, unable to come up with anything. I was starting to fear that we might not be able to do it. In the meantime the feeding tube was causing more and more problems. She regularly had small amounts of blood coming from her stomach. It was becoming harder and harder to place a feeding tube when one had to be replaced, or when she pulled it out again.

Still we did accomplish something. Although she was still not eating, within a month she was starting to become much more active. She was moving her arms and legs about when lying on the floor, rolling onto her side. Relaxing and using her right arm and hand more and more and smiling freely. That in itself was already a lot gained. She was enjoying life more. Not just in short moments, but most of the time.

Then, mid-August, we brought three babies to hospital for liver tests. Two of them were newly arrived babies, who needed to be checked for hepatitis, since they had stayed in a *fuliyuan*. Lili was the third one, she needed the test because she was taking Depakine against seizures and this can cause liver problems. All three babies had not been allowed to eat since four o'clock in the morning, because the test had to be done on an empty stomach. The two little ones were screaming in protest over their empty stomachs. Lili did not seem to experience the slightest discomfort. It appeared that she was not really aware of a hunger sensation.

Halfway to the hospital, quick as a flash Lili moved her hand and before I realised what she had done, she had pulled out her feeding tube. The end of it had already hardened too much to be able to reinsert it, and we had not brought along a new feeding tube. So for the moment there was little we could do. We went to hospital, had the blood drawn and gave the famished babies their bottles. I tried to feed Lili with the sipping cup we had brought. She took 8 mls. Still she did not complain at all.

The coming together of circumstances: the discovery that Lili did not seem to suffer from hunger, the fact that she was rather fat and thus had some reserves – though how she did get fat is a mystery, she was certainly not overfed

–, the damage that the feeding tube was doing and the sheer desperation over whether we would ever succeed in getting her to feed orally lead me to make a radical decision. I decided not to place a new feeding tube when we got back to WEST, but to try if we could get her to take milk orally. In this case, since Lili seemed unaware of hunger, the absence of back up was certainly much more of a motivator for me than for her. Whichever way though, it worked.

Again, like with Yan before, initially I was the only one allowed to feed her. At Sun's suggestion I tried using a Haberman feeder, the only kind of nipple I had not yet tried on Lili. She took it. To start with she ate about twenty minutes out of every hour. But her intake increased every time. The first time 15 ml, the next hour already 30ml. And so on. Once she reached 50ml, I started feeding her every other hour, which gave both her and me some breathing space in between feeds. With her steady improvement, but on the other hand still difficult, labour intensive feeding, I was not ready yet to hand over when evening came. So I was prepared to get up every two hours through the night.

Nighttime turned out to be a completely different matter, however. Lili had never learned to make a connection between feeding and being awake. While she used the feeding tube, she received 80ml of formula every two hours, around the clock regardless of whether she was awake or asleep. When I came to feed her at midnight, she was more or less awake, since she had just been given her medication, but after drinking about 15 ml, she fell asleep again and was impossible to rouse. Two hours later, she was sleeping like a log, and nothing I did by way of touching, holding her up, patting her back, letting her feel the nipple or talking to her would make her stir in any way at all. There was no waking her.

So I went back to bed and asked them to call me if she woke up at any stage. When I woke up myself, it was almost 6 in the morning. I immediately went over to the baby home and found Lili waking up. I was told they were just about to call me. This second day, again she was constantly improving the volume of her intake. Plus not having the feeding tube there, appeared to improve her whole outlook on life. She did not enjoy eating, but she did do it. In between feeds she was more and more cheerful and outgoing.

That night I gave her a midnight feed again, slightly more than before, and managed to get a little bit more into her around 4am. By sheer willpower and constant stimulation. Energy needed to be expended not only in getting Lili to eat, but also in fighting off the substitute shift supervisor who was manning the nightshift. A woman known to me more for her great efforts in making a good impression than in her effort in doing her job properly. She was constantly harassing me by telling me to go to bed, that she was well able to feed Lili, that I should be resting etc. – that is what I mean by the good impression making, showing constant concern over my well being, rather than that of the babies. In fact I knew that of all the caregivers present, she was probably the one least able to feed Lili. In the end I told her bluntly that if I found out that anyone other than myself had fed Lili, I would be livid. That put an end to that. I was proven right about her, a few days later.

On the third day of Lili eating by herself, we had another baby who was in very bad shape and getting weaker and weaker. The day before he had been dehydrated. But now that that was solved, his overall condition was not improving. In fact when I was called out of bed at half past four in the morning, it did not look like he would live another hour. I decided we would wait to see if he would make it until five o'clock, if he did, we would take him to hospital to see if there was anything they could do for him there.

He did in fact make it until then, so I told Hai to go and get dressed quickly, I would do the same when she came back and then we would go. The shift supervisor on duty, one of the nuns, baptised the baby and after she had organised all his things to take into hospital she suggested she call Sun, because 'it might be handy to have her around at the hospital'. I was grateful for this offer. Both because of the support that Sun would in fact be able to give at the hospital, and because this was clearly said to me to indicate that I was not the only one who thought that Hai would be absolutely useless there.

When the call was made, Hai had still not returned. I handed the baby to the shift supervisor and went to change from my pyjamas into my clothes in about two minutes, finding Hai having an elaborate wash in the bathroom. Sun, who had been called out of bed and had to walk over from home, arrived at the baby home at about the same time Hai did, who only had to walk over to the apartment next door before the call was ever made.

When we arrived at the hospital the baby's condition had improved somewhat. The doctor did not think it necessary to admit him and did think he would be all right to travel to EAST on the train. So it was decided that I would take him that noon. This was not an easy decision to make for me, because it would mean handing over Lili's feeding, something I was loath to do at this early stage. On the other hand the baby going to EAST was in such a fragile condition that I was also unwilling to let him be taken by just an *ayi*.

I decided to go to EAST, and hand picked *ayi* who would be allowed to feed Lili on the different shifts. In a way it was probably good that the situation forced me to hand over her feeding, because it had to be done at some stage and it would be very hard to do at any time. She drank quite well in my absence, especially doing better at night than I had been able to get her to. The baby I brought to EAST made it there all right, but passed away the following morning.

Lili's feeding was not entirely out of my hands yet, however. There were certain *ayi* who were very good with her and got her to drink much better than I could. However there were many who were not up to the task. Lili has never enjoyed drinking. She fights it and needs constant encouragement and entertainment in order to have her continue drinking. Feeds would usually take something along the lines of 45 minutes. Thankfully because her intake improved, she was eventually, after a week or two, able to take about 150 ml, which meant she only needed to eat once every four hours, allowing her longer 'torture-free' periods.

Especially for night feeds it was hard to find people able to give her enough. For the first few weeks, on the night shift I arranged for the shift supervisors to feed her, since the *ayi* were not up to it. Then came the two nights when the substitute shift supervisor was in charge again. The one who had assured me she was well able to feed Lili. I decided to give her a chance and let her try. I walked in at midnight and found her holding Lili, who was half awake, trying to wake her up more. I explained to her that there was no point in waking her up more, that she needed to get as much milk into the child as possible right now, while she was still half awake. The supervisor mumbled something in acknowledgement and kept right on trying to rouse Lili. After one more comment and no response, I took Lili from her and fed her myself. I only managed to get about 24 ml into her before she was sound asleep again, but that was better than nothing.

Still people deserve chances, and now she had seen how to do it, the next night feed was up to her. When I got up at six, just before the end of her shift, to see how she had done, I found the second night feed had been skipped. The reason given was that Lili had been too sleepy. Of course she was sleepy! It is damn near impossible to rouse her, but when you get any kind of response you immediately put the nipple in her mouth and keep working on her! This was a big problem. Not just because of the intake missed during the night, which for the moment never amounted to a great deal anyway. It was because of the knock on effect. We were starting to find out that when Lili skipped a night feed, in other words when the gap between two feeds was too great, she fed very poorly in the morning. It was as if she then forgot what she was supposed to do again.

So the following night, the second one of this particular woman's shift, I set my alarm again and fed her myself. I swept the – numerous – protestations about her being able to do it and my needing my rest aside. I plainly stated that rest would be nice, but that since she had had a chance and had proven she was incapable of feeding Lili, I did not have much choice but to get up and feed her myself.

Situations like this made me incredibly angry and sad. Not on my own behalf, over having to get up during the night. But for the sake of Lili. She had worked so hard and had come so far. Still the danger that she would one day suddenly throw in the towel again, was still present. People antagonising her or not treating her properly surrounding feeds, made it more likely that she would. I felt so strongly she did not deserve that. After all she had been through and all she had accomplished she did not deserve having to have a feeding tube placed again. Also I was fairly sure that if a feeding tube would ever be placed again, we would probably not succeed in getting her off it.

Over time more and more *ayi* learned to feed Lili and many of them got better results than I did. But there always remained a few who seemed incapable of grasping the concept of encouraging a child. They would constantly criticize and admonish her for drinking slowly, instead of praising her for doing well. Something, which Lili is particularly sensitive to.

The second half of September I took two weeks off. The first time I had a holiday since I had arrived in China. In that time I wanted to see a little bit more of the country, but on the other hand I also desperately needed rest. Just recharging before going 'back into battle' again. The time that I was away, two people from higher management in EAST – one week each – came to WEST to assist Hai. Another indication to me that it was not just a personal dislike on my part, which was causing the problems with her. Normally substitution was only arranged if the children's home director herself had to be absent for more than a day.

So I went and saw some of the sights, such as the terracotta army at Xi'an, I climbed Hua Shan, a mountain east of Xi'an and visited the Tibetan Buddhist Labrang monastery in Xiahe. But most of my afternoons I spend napping or reading on my bed, catching up on some rest. I also found that I was still very much preoccupied with the babies in WEST.

When I came back from my holidays at the end of September, I was soon back in exactly the same patterns. I really felt I could not go on like that anymore, with regards to Hai. So after a few days, I announced that mid October I would come to EAST to talk things through and to try and find a solution. I had been thinking about possible alternatives to present during my vacation.

I felt that in order for me to be able to stay in WEST something needed to change. I could not stay if things did not improve. There were two options, that I could see, which would make my existence more bearable. One was that Hai would be replaced completely and thus the whole situation changed. The second one was to make me officially responsible for the medical goings on in WEST, not just de facto. This would mean that Hai would no longer be allowed to make any medical decisions – eliminating my worry about what she might be doing in my absence – and it would allow me to communicate directly with EAST about medical cases, so I would know the information passed on was correct.

I had a meeting with the CEO. He said he agreed with my opinion about Hai, but there were two other people in higher management who felt that there might still be a chance that she would improve. He wanted to give them a chance to prove this. Which was fair enough. So for the moment she was not going anywhere.

The second option he felt was not really worth the trouble, because at the end of the month a new position would commence, that of Care Manager. Hua was back from maternity leave and being trained in EAST in more medical skills for the position. This position would start in all the location and basically the Care Manager would be fulfilling the function which I had created around me over time, that of medical overseer, only this would be for both children's home and foster care in any given location. The Care Manager would also be the liaison with the *fuliyuan*. Which would effectively reduce the position of children's home director to an administrative and logistic one – these were things that Hai was now handling reasonably well. Since this would all be changing around in only a few weeks time, there was not much point in making big structural changes in the set up at this point. Which I thought was a valid point.

So for me it was hereby decided that I would not be staying on at WEST. The alternative options were to either be placed at NORTH - the volunteer who had been there, had left in August - or EAST, or to rotate. The CEO was open to either option and left it up to me to decide. I decided to opt for rotating, going around all three locations – now soon to be four locations, as SOUTH was by now in concrete preparation –, staying about two weeks in any one location. There were only three more months left in my stay in China, so to spend much more time in any one location, would barely allow any rotating.

I felt that by rotating, spending some time in each location, I would have an opportunity to help teach and train staff in the various things I had picked up along the way and which I had already been implementing in WEST. Thus helping make improvements everywhere and getting to know more about all the locations. Another reason for choosing rotation was that it would allow me to go back to WEST for periods as well. Although I was fleeing from Hai, I did not want to break off completely from the good friends and lovely children that I had there, whom I would miss terribly.

This proposal was approved. I knew I was doing the right thing, and to a certain extent I was looking forward to going from place to place, meeting new challenges. Still it was not easy and tears had to be shed at the prospect of leaving WEST, which really did feel like home to me.

I travelled back to WEST at the same time as Hai, who had just had a week's holiday, and stopped by EAST before returning. In the car to the train station I announced that I would be in WEST one more week and then I would be going to NORTH. This was met with an 'oh, really'. 'Yes,' I said, 'from now on, I will be rotating, spending two weeks in every location.' Her reaction to this was: 'Before the children's home directors rotated too, but now they don't anymore.' – this had in fact been changed. I told her that I knew that but that I had chosen myself to rotate. Here she grabbed back at what I said before and commented that two weeks was really too short a time to stay in one place, I should ask for longer periods.

I was becoming rather exasperated. It appeared I really needed to spell it out for her. I did, telling her that we both knew that our relationship was not very good and that I could not stay in WEST any longer. She said in surprise that just because our characters were not the same that was no reason for me to ruin the last three months I had left in China. At that point I knew I had made the right decision. I could never work with her. I did try to explain further, but I do not think she understood at all.

Back at WEST the reactions were more heart-warming and understanding. Even though I never told anyone but Sun about the real reasons behind the decision. To others it had simply been decided in EAST that I would rotate to train people in all locations. Despite all my problems with Hai, I have always done my best not to have confrontations in front of other staff and I never discussed it with anyone. Because at the end of the day she is their director and it does not help if I undermine her authority.

Not that there was much need for that. Whenever someone asked me what they were to do when I would be gone, I answered that Hai would still be there. Usually this would get me a look, or an outright derogatory comment. To which my only added response was to mention that Sun would still be there too, that was acknowledged as a relief.

To Sun I did explain, she was also the only person who knew why I had gone to EAST. She understood my reasons, but still did not hold back in saying that she really did not like it that I was going. I took her out to dinner on my last evening, though I ended up not being allowed to pay afterwards.

So at the end of October I got on the train to NORTH, together with Lili, who was now eating so well, solids as well as formula, that she was able to 'go home'. So at least I would not have to miss all of the babies, I got to keep her with me a little while longer.

Turning 30

At WEST I had learned most of the things I knew connected with what I did in the children's homes. I had slowly built up a reputation and over time people turned to me for help more and more and were more inclined to do what I asked without questioning. This was something I did not take for granted. In fact, it still surprised me from time to time that things I said were acted on immediately without question.

In NORTH I had no such history to draw on. In fact I did not have a history there at all. The children's home director there, Ping, was new and I had never met her before. Imagine my surprise when I stepped into the NORTH baby home for the first time – to get Lili settled in her new home, on arrival –, had a look around, did not agree with the way some things were being handled, commented on them and found that adjustments were made straight away. That really blew me away.

From the moment I set foot in NORTH I was running, constantly. Since the director here was new, she too still had a lot to learn. The big difference between Ping and Hai was that Ping was very eager to learn and learned fast, which made that part of life a lot more enjoyable for me. Ironically, the relationship with the care supervisor – one that I was used to being extremely smooth going with Sun – was a lot more problematic here.

The lady who at that time still held that position in NORTH, Xiu, did not have much affinity with children, it soon became clear to me. She especially did not like children who had serious problems, they just complicated our lives. Probably mainly because of her disinterest, I soon discovered quite a lot of ways in which her work was not up to scratch, leading to a lower level of care for the children, since it was her job to oversee this.

As it happened NORTH did not often have babies with serious problems, at least never for a long time, as they were more likely to be sent to EAST sooner than those in WEST. At this particular moment however, there was a baby with a heart defect and very severe pneumonia who seemed unlikely to have very long to live. It was too big a risk to put her on a train.

The day after I arrived we received four new babies from the *fuliyuan*, one of them was very emaciated and her breathing was very difficult. I will call her Min. The first evening she stayed at NORTH she looked like she would not make it through the night, Ping and I stayed up with her until half past four when she stabilized more or less. In the first week she stayed at NORTH, it happened three times that we were all but certain that Min had only a few more hours to live, her breathing became that difficult. While this was something, which concerned and moved most of us, it mostly annoyed Xiu.

A week after Min's arrival both she and the baby with pneumonia were using the oxygen concentrator, when the power was suddenly cut at 9.30 in the morning, with no warning. In this case we did not have an oxygen bottle present as back up. The two girls were suddenly on their own for their breathing. Ping immediately got on the phone. She found out that the power would not return until 16.30, so we were faced by 7 hours with no oxygen. Min's condition was already starting to deteriorate. While the director tried everything she could to organise someway for us to give the girls oxygen, I held Min, sitting by the other girl's bed, monitoring them both.

Because Ping had only started work at NORTH a month before, she turned to Xiu– who had worked there for several years – for advice on who to contact and where to go for help. A natural thing to do. The care supervisor's response was: 'It's no use.' The tone in her voice clearly indicating that if the two babies would just go ahead and die, that would make all of our lives that much easier. We were aghast when we heard that. However at that moment, we did not have time to pause. Ping used her own wits and managed to arrange permission from the little clinic around the corner for us to come and sit there with the two babies and have them hooked up to their oxygen bottle.

The whole process of organising this took about an hour in total. In that time Min's oxygen saturation had reached 24%. A normal saturation is 95-99% and aside from her I have never seen a baby reach 24% and recover, usually a saturation that low is only seen in a steadily downward trend.

We bundled up the babies and a bag of essentials and half ran to the clinic, where they were put on oxygen again. The baby with pneumonia looked a lot better straight away. Min improved somewhat, for a while, but her breathing was still very difficult. I sat holding Min and Xiu held the other baby. For a little while that was. Before long she started complaining that the baby was too heavy to be holding all the time and she put her down on the bed she was sitting on.

As always in public situations, we quickly had quite a crowd gathered around. Two babies a*nd* a foreigner! That is a spectacle too good to miss. Everyone had their own comments or advice about the situation. *Ayi* were running back and forth between the children's home and the clinic with bottles of milk and medication etc.

Min looked increasingly weak and her colour was not good. Even though she was now back on oxygen, it was possible that having been off it for an hour had already caused too much damage for her to recover again. At about two in the afternoon Ping came to take over from me, so that I could go and have something to eat. I ran to the office apartment, shoved some food into me and ran back again. When I walked into the clinic again, I was immediately struck by Min's grey colour, a very bad sign. It did not look like she would make it.

What was worse than Min probably not being able to survive, was that the doctor at the clinic was extremely agitated and nervous. Repeating over and over again that Min was not doing well, that it was not going well at all. We might potentially get into a lot of trouble – worst case scenario being the entire foundation in China being shut down – if we were perceived as just having sat there doing nothing while a baby was dying and that was reported to the authorities.

I quietly discussed this with Ping and suggested that we take Min back to the children's home. We could not provide her with oxygen there, but it looked like even on oxygen, she did not have much longer to go, and it could prevent a lot of problems. Ping called her superior in EAST to ask for permission, who in turn asked to speak to me. She asked me whether I was quite sure there was nothing we could do for the baby. All I answered was 'She is grey', to which she immediately responded: 'Take her out of there!'

So we made it seem like we were going to take Min to hospital and left a disgruntled care supervisor behind with the other baby. It was about three o'clock when we arrived back at the children's home with Min. I connected her to the pulse/oximeter to be able to monitor her heart rate and oxygen levels. That was just giving the first reading, when all of a sudden the power came back on, an hour and a half early. We immediately put Min back on oxygen and by some miracle, she actually survived. Ping and I felt triumph and relief. Xiu, who had been called to come back, now that we had power again, did not seem to feel anything much.

The next day, while I was sitting with Min, suddenly all the pieces fell together in my head and I finally realised that she had Pierre-Robin sequence. I had never actually seen anyone who had that condition before, but I did know – from reading up on it – how it presented. I wanted to kick myself for not realising this before. Once we knew that this was her problem, we knew Min needed to always be in a prone position to prevent her tongue from slipping back and blocking her airways. From that moment on, she was never turned over again, even having her nappies changed while lying prone and suddenly she was stable. She did not crash again. Feeding was not a problem, since she was being fed by feeding tube already anyway. That can be done prone just as well as supine.

Once she was stable for a couple of days, we decided to take the risk and bring Min to EAST on a 15-hour train journey. I would be the one to take her. Another *ayi* would come along and bring her roommate, whose pneumonia had improved a lot, so that we now thought she would be able to survive the train journey.

We arranged a large oxygen bottle, so that we were able to provide the girls with oxygen during the trip. But that was not the biggest hurdle. When we arrived at the train station, with the two babies, their things and the big oxygen bottle on a trolley, we were stopped. They did not want to give us permission to board with the oxygen bottle. We put up a big dramatic scene – which although possibly slightly over-acted, was in essence true – about the babies having to get on the train, because they needed surgery in the city at the other end. That without the oxygen they could not survive the journey. That without the surgery they could not survive full stop and how were they going to get the surgery if they could not get on the train? Making sure to show Min, who was tiny, skin and bones, exactly the kind of image you would use to melt your way into someone's heart.

Meanwhile time was ticking and the train would arrive very soon. After a long and heated debate, we were allowed onto the platform, but it still had not been decided whether or not we would be let onto the train. They then proposed that we would upgrade our tickets to first class: soft sleepers, that way we would be in a closed compartment and no one would see us – and more importantly the oxygen bottle. We were not willing to spend the fortune needed to upgrade however. It was like a stand off. The train arrived, people got off, people got on, still nothing.

Then all of a sudden the officials shouted at us that we had to hurry and get on because the train was about to leave. So we bustled on, with babies, bags and oxygen bottle. A quick goodbye to Ping – since I had been there almost two weeks, it had been decided I might as well rotate to EAST now that I was heading there anyway, instead of coming back again for two days - and she had to run to get off the train in time.

People were cleared out of the bunks above us, moved to different places. Which did not serve much of a purpose, because crowds would gather around us from other bunks anyway. But if that made them feel happier and if that allowed us on the train, who were we to argue.

With Min having to lie prone, for most of the 15 hours, I lay back on my bunk, with her lying on my chest. Apart from the breathing difficulties, Min also had the strange tendency to have a high temperature – not a fever, an actual elevated body temperature – whenever you put clothes or covers on her. So she lay there wearing only a short-sleeved vest, covering her nappy. At one point during the journey, a lady passed by and saw me lying there with the tiny baby on my chest – with feeding tube and oxygen tube hanging off her. She then asked if I had just given birth to the baby. Which I thought was quite hysterical. Min is still alive and doing well today.

While in NORTH, I criticised many aspects of the care supervisor's job there, which were performed at nowhere near an acceptable standard. She resented me terribly for making her life more complicated and for making her work hard. She was there not for doing the job, but for holding the 'title'. Xiu relished the status and esteem that it gave her, putting her above everyone else – apart from the director. While I was not out to humiliate her, only to improve the quality of care, she did perceive what I did as exactly that.

On two occasions she tried to bring me down. Waiting to have as many people present as possible to witness the event, she would question something I said in a tone, which clearly said 'If you would just think for a moment you would realise how stupid what you just said is'. This backfired badly however, because each time I calmly explained to her why what I was saying did make sense and why I wanted things done that way. Both times she made her retreat like a beaten dog, having lost face and resenting me even more. She realised this was not the way to go, so she stopped doing it.

At EAST I reported her behaviour and the ways in which her work was far below standard to higher management. They agreed with me, but needed to think of a way to get rid of her without giving her any leeway for vindictive behaviour – something we all knew to beware of in her. One option proposed by the CEO was to just eliminate the position of care supervisor, she could not really do much about that, in EAST the position was already gone. At this I asked 'What about Sun?' He grinned and told me not to worry, they did not want to get rid of Sun; they would just call her position something else and let her continue as she was.

As it happened, we did not need to do anything. The day after I arrived at EAST the person in charge of all directors told me that Xiu had asked the director to be allowed to work as normal caregiver, as she was 'no longer comfortable' in her job. This again was a ploy of her. It is possible that in some way she was afraid, knowing what I thought of her and that I was now at EAST talking to management. Mostly however it was probably a stab at the Ping, whom she did not get on with very well either, because she was not afraid to stand up to Xiu. The basic idea probably being that management would be aghast that the inexperienced little director could have caused our wonderful care supervisor to want to lay down her job. Unfortunately for her, this little plan backfired as well. We were cheering!

The next day Xiu called the director's manager directly to let her know that she had 'special reasons for her decision'. The director's manager listen very 'sympathetically' and told her she would have to wait until a decision was made at the management meeting on Monday. I got a full report of the conversation, and again of the one, which followed the management meeting. The director's manager called Xiu to let her know they had decided to 'give her permission' to work as an *ayi* from then on. After which the former care supervisor said nothing, there was nothing she could say. She was put on the night shift.

When I was at NORTH again two weeks later, I had to use all I had not to laugh or make any comments, when I walked into the baby home in the evening and saw her wearing the regular *ayi* uniform. I managed it, though. I had no desire to kick her while she was down.

At EAST I was quite busy as well, since at the time there were quite a few babies who were in serious condition both in the foundation's children's homes and at the hospice. So I spent my time running between the four EAST apartments and the hospice. Sitting with whoever was in the worse shape at any given time. Going mostly from one crashing baby to the next.

I was at EAST a few days, when my 30th birthday arrived. I have never had any angst about getting older and reaching milestones. For me my thirtieth birthday was just the one, which came after the twenty-ninth. According to many people this is supposed to be a day to never forget. It is made memorable by huge birthday parties and such things. I did not have a big party, but still my 30th birthday is certainly one to remember forever.

It started like all other days, doing the rounds of the four homes, taking care of babies. I was invited for lunch with the people who run the hospice. That was really nice. Complete with a muffin with a candle in it. The people there were all about my age, younger or older by a year perhaps. So we had great laughs about the fact that I was 30 now and still single. In China if you have not found a partner by 30 you are considered an old maid and all hope of ever finding someone is out the window. From then on you can start preparing yourself for an old age with no one to take care of you. We commented that it was a great relief that hope was now finally out of the window and that at least now I knew where I stood.

After lunch it was back to work. That afternoon, something momentous, in a small way, did happen. The very first time I ever set foot in one of the children's homes, back in January, I first walked up to a baby who was sitting in a high chair, with big rosy cheeks, lets call him Xiong. I chatted to him and moved to touch him, or pick him up or something, and he immediately screamed as if I was going to kill him. He obviously was not fond of strangers. So I moved away from him and sat with a little girl who smiled at me straight away.

In the ten months that had passed, this boy had still never allowed me to get near him. He had always remained scared of me somehow. Perhaps because I am white. The day before my birthday Xiong was not doing well at all. In one day, he crashed three times. Going very dark purple, hardly breathing. One of the times I was there when it happened and every time we had been able to bring him back. But we were not very hopeful that he would live very long. He only had half a heart.

On my birthday Xiong was doing very well again. His colour was – relatively – good, he was happy and lively, starting to say words. Most amazingly, he indicated that he wanted to be held by me. For the first time in all those months. He sat on my arm for a few minutes, smiling and chatting, before choosing someone else he wanted to go to. I was really touched by that.

At the end of the afternoon, I went to the special care unit, where Wang, a baby boy with a heart condition was not doing well at all. He looked greyish blue and had crashed a few times during the day. It seemed almost certain that he would not live out the day. It almost seemed suiting to me. It was my birthday, the middle of life, I knew that a friend of mine in Europe was having a baby delivered by c-section that day, the start of life, and here would be an end to life too, in all likelihood. I sat with Wang for about half an hour, before I needed to go.

I had been invited to have dinner with the CEO and his family and some mutual friends, for my birthday. That was the start of an eventful evening. While five of us were in the car on the way to the house, the hospice director got a phone call from EAST if she could come over and help out, because Xiong had crashed again and needed to be brought over to the special care unit. She replied that she was not on the compound at the moment, and then I heard her say that I was not there either, because we were all on our way together. I felt very sorry for the EAST Care Manager, who was there having to deal with it without our help now.

We arrived and had a cheerful start to the evening. Until during dinner we were notified that Xiong had passed away. Because he had been doing so much better that day, this came as quite a shock. Shortly after the hospice director was asked to come to EAST, because they needed to bring Xiong to the hospital to get a death certificate and meanwhile Wang looked like he was about to go too. She left immediately, with her friend. Twenty minutes after Xiong, Wang passed away too.

We still had some cake, but the festive mood was certainly gone now. Not long after, I received a text message from the hospice director's friend asking me to come to the hospice when I returned to the compound. The hospice director had gone to hospital with Wang for his death certificate, and her friend had gone to check on the babies in the hospice. As soon as the CEO returned from bringing the two of them to the compound, I got in the car with him and made my way to the hospice.

There the three month old boy with a heart condition and pneumonia, Wen, who had been at death's door for a few days now – and two days before had seemed on death's threshold – had crashed again and was breathing very hard. We sat with him for about three hours, after which the others all got back from the crematorium. It was about midnight now. By this time Wen had stabilized more or less. We stood there talking for a while about everything that had happened that evening. Then we broke up, most of us going to our dorms to get some sleep.

I was not able to sleep just yet. I needed to unwind a little first. So I got something to drink and my laptop. I wrote my daily report and had a look at some emails and stuff. Just before one o'clock I got a call from the hospice. Hao, a girl with spina bifida who had been very pale and unlike herself the past few days, seemed to be going downhill. I turned off my laptop and rushed over.

Hao was in fact whiter than white and her breathing irregular. We sat with her for about an hour. Then she seemed to stabilize again. Most of the people who had been called in went back to try and get some sleep. I decided to stay this time, together with another lady – apart of course from the normal caregivers. Not long after the others had gone, Wen started going downhill again. I sat with him. Still we held off on calling everyone in, since he was starting to get a reputation for looking like he was about to die, keeping that up for hours and then recovering again.

After forty-five minutes to an hour however he really seemed to be choking, so I had the other lady pull everyone out of bed again. They came and Wen improved after about half an hour. So most went back to bed. The hospice director decided to stay a bit longer. She went to look at Hao and found that she was drenched in sweat. So she washed Hao down and changed her clothes, to make her more comfortable. Suddenly Hao started to fade fast. Everyone was called out of bed again. We all sat around, with the two babies both in a terrible state, it seemed impossible to predict who would go first.

Just after four o'clock, Hao passed away. Wen seemed like he only had minutes to live as well, and we all encouraged him to let go and to go together with his 'sister'. But he kept on hanging on. The car came and the hospice director and her friend took Hao to the hospital for her death certificate and then to the crematorium. When they returned at about half past seven in the morning, Wen still looked just as likely to die in the next couple of minutes as he had several hours ago.

We stayed around for a little longer, but by now we were all dizzy with exhaustion. So we decided to break up and get some sleep, with the exception of one person. I went to bed at eight in the morning, fully expected to get a call any moment. At a quarter past nine my phone rang. I was so dazed with exhaustion and sleep that I was convinced it was the hospice and I could not even recognise the voice on the other end. The cheerful: 'Hello birthday girl, are you still in bed?!' did not break through my consciousness, I just asked 'How is he?'. Which in turn caused confusion, because I was in fact talking to the director's manager, who had no idea that I had only just gone to bed, nor who on earth I was talking about. She just called to ask if I could give some visiting doctors a tour of EAST. When she realised I was only just asleep, she said she would arrange someone else.

I was awake for half an hour after that, but then I did manage to sleep again for just over an hour. After that I got up, attended the EAST medical meeting and then returned to the hospice, where Wen still looked like he would go any moment now. Everyone was starting to gather there again, after a couple of hours sleep.

Wen managed to hold on until almost five o'clock in the afternoon, I stayed there until that time. I feel blessed to have been able to be present that day. It was such a beautiful, serene atmosphere. Despite the exhaustion and the battle against death that was going on. We took turns holding Wen, and the others gathered around. Sometimes praying, sometimes singing, sometimes talking and even laughing. The other children in the hospice were included, when they wanted to. Allowed to sit on their preferred person's lap and be a part of it. It was amazing. When Wen finally decided to let go, it was a great relief. Both for him and for us.

That evening I was asked the inevitable question: 'So, how does it feel to be thirty?' My answer was: 'I did not think it would make any difference, but I have never felt this tired in my entire life. So something must have changed!'

Although technically two of the babies died after midnight of my birthday, to me my thirtieth birthday will always be the day on which we lost four babies in 24 hours. Something, which also there is extremely rare. It is certainly a day I will never forget. But something which I cannot stress enough is that is was not a bad or horrible day. It was very intense, but in many ways beautiful too.

While I still had two months left in China, after my birthday and I continued to work very hard – while it seemed impossible, in fact still increasingly hard, for instance afternoon naps were completely gone now, I could not imagine anymore how I had ever found the time for them – and with dedication, in some way it was starting to be the unwinding towards the end. I think this is largely due to two things. One was that I needed to start arranging my journey back to Europe, book tickets and arrange the three visas needed to return by Transsiberian Express. The other reason I think was that I was no longer living at WEST, which meant that in a way part of the goodbye had already been said. Even though I continued to learn and enjoy what I was doing.

Saying Goodbye

After my two weeks at EAST I was requested to go back to NORTH instead of going on to WEST, because there were some issues at NORTH, which they wanted me to help out with. I agreed to go there for a week. I was longing to see WEST again, finally. The week at NORTH was of course not uneventful, it was frantically busy, but as time goes by, you adjust your standards and I had come to see weeks like these are more or less run of the mill. It was the last time I visited NORTH, and the hardest thing about leaving was having to say goodbye to Lili, who had come very close to my heart.

Arriving back at WEST was wonderful. I arrived very early in the morning and when I went to the baby home at about six o'clock, I was greeted with a hug by the shift supervisor. The same when Sun arrived at work two hours later. It really felt like coming home again. Now that Hai had a Care Manager over her, I was able to stay out of her way most of the time and deal with Hua instead. Which worked very well.

The two weeks I spend at WEST were very hectic. In that space of time I travelled back and forth to EAST twice, with babies in very fragile conditions. I would have gone a third time, only I was not allowed. Because of my being a foreigner, I was not allowed to travel on my own with babies who were particularly weak. It was these babies I insisted on taking myself, because if something went wrong on the way, I might be able to do something to help them which *ayi* would not be able to do – for instance I have on several occasions placed feeding tubes while on the road, and once have given an antibiotics injection. However if help would turn out not to suffice and the baby would not make it, I would be a foreigner with a dead Chinese baby, something which could cause enormous problems. So whenever I travelled with an at-risk baby, an *ayi* had to accompany me, whether she had her 'own' baby to care for or not.

So that in case things went wrong, the dead baby could be handed to a Chinese person. Thankfully it never came to that while I was in China, but it was not unthinkable.

In the case of the third baby in those two weeks needing to go to EAST, it was not possible to arrange for someone to come with me. The baby was a tiny premature girl, with unstable body temperature. In the end it was decided that Sun – the only person I trusted to give the same level of care as I would – would take this baby. It was a good thing too that it was not a regular *ayi* taking her, because the baby became hypothermic again, on the way, and Sun managed to remedy that.

One of the things, which delighted me tremendously about being at WEST, was being able to work with Sun again. It was marvellous to instantly fall back into the same effortless cooperation, complementing each other and getting things done. Unfortunately we were not to enjoy this very long. I was there not quite a week, when Sun rang one evening to let us know her father-in-law was not doing well at all, there was a problem with his heart and he had to go to hospital. So she and her husband needed to travel over straight away to take care of him and see how he was. Her father-in-law passed away a couple of days later, and Sun returned after all the mourning rituals had been gone through, a few days after I had left WEST again. So while I was still there I got to take care of both sides of our two-woman-ship.

From WEST I travelled to SOUTH, the newly opened children's home, further to the southwest. Here I was reunited with Jian. It was great to catch up with her again.

My stay at SOUTH turned out to be a short one, however. I was only there two and a half days, before I travelled to EAST again, with a critically ill baby – and of course an *ayi* and another baby. We travelled by night train, the baby got worse on the train, before he started to improve slightly towards dawn. So I was not granted any sleep. We arrived – with delay – in a white city, it was snowing. Something, which is quite rare, as winters at EAST are very, very dry.

As I was only planning to stay at SOUTH for a week before moving on to EAST, and the travel time was very long, I did not return. So that was my hello and goodbye to SOUTH in one. It was the last time I met Jian. The day after I left SOUTH, Jian got sick and needed to go into hospital for quite some time. The EAST Care manager was sent to SOUTH to take over from her, and I took over from the Care manager at EAST for the next two and a half weeks. Keeping me well occupied. This even included evaluating shift supervisors' technical knowledge – of the medical equipment they are supposed to know how to use – together with the director's manager and the medical director.

Just before Christmas, I finally managed to make a short trip to the Great Wall. One part of it is not that far away from EAST, but still I had never visited it, in all the time I had by now spent in China. It was nice to finally see it for real. Although I still feel that the sight of the wall snaking its way through the landscape, over the mountains is much more impressive than actually being on it.

My Christmas at EAST consisted of attending a dinner on Christmas Eve and afterward an illegal midnight mass. Christmas day was work as usual, with a call via Skype to my parents in the evening – which was the middle of the day in Europe. The next day I was on a train to WEST again. China does not really know Christmas. So it is only the foreigners who hold some celebrations. It was certainly a different Christmas.

Then came my very last week at WEST. A week, which mixed enjoyment of being there again, normal hard work, and sadness at the impending goodbye. Moments of realisation occasionally piercing a vast sea of obliviousness.

Another surreal experience was New Year. We see this as a big thing in the West, a new year starting. It seems so real. In China however it has no meaning. It just means that you throw out the old calendar and put up a new one. The real new year is the Lunar Chinese New Year. So I did stay up until midnight, out of principle mainly. But I was the only one to do so. I went into the baby home, to at least have some people around me. There I picked up Yur, who had woken up for the occasion and she was the one I wished a happy New Year when the time came. No one else seemed to notice or care that 2008 had begun.

Two days before I would definitely leave, the care manager and the children's home director had organised the monthly general staff meeting, which this time would be a combination of staff meeting, new years greeting and goodbye party for me. Days in advance, the *ayi* were writing and practising songs in my honour, with the babies on their laps.

The meeting, as always, was held in two parts, since there always needed to be people to take care of the children. So the meetings were held before and after 14.00, which was when the shift change takes place. This time I, of course, had to be there for both.

They became lovely gatherings, everyone had to sing. There were songs made in my honour, which I found very touching. But also other, existing songs were sung. I was made to sing one song in Dutch and one in English, for exotic effect. For an English song I chose 'The Parting Glass', which fitted the occasion perfectly. Then there was a lot of fun and games.

I gave every member of the staff a small gift, which I had prepared for the occasion. I had bought 60 sets of chopsticks. On every set I wrote my Chinese name at the top of one chopstick, and the name of the staff member at the top of the other. The two sticks were then tied together with a red string. The idea behind this being that one chopstick – representing the one person – is relatively useless, but when you have the two together, they become extremely useful.

At the end of the first meeting, they sang one last song, made for me, all together. While this was being sung, a shift supervisor came forward and embraced me. They then continued to sing the song again and again, while one by one everyone came forward to say goodbye. A lot of tears were shed during these proceedings. Finally a group photo was taken and that was the end of the meeting.

The second meeting was much the same as the first; only some people had prepared dance as well as song this time. And at the end there was no emotional goodbye. Which shows the influence of a single individual in setting something like that in motion. Part of it probably was too that the second meeting had a lot of people from the night shift who do not know me as well as those who work during the day. Since I was only present at night in case of an emergency.

After that, it was back to work for another day and a half. Now I was decidedly feeling like I was moving towards the end, and rather dreading it. One of the last nights at WEST Hai gave one last demonstration of how finely attuned she was to those around her. Everyone knew that I was very sad to be about to leave WEST and, shortly after, China. The two of us were in the office by ourselves, when she suddenly remarked: 'You will be going home very soon now. You must be so happy!' After I had blinked and let it sink in that she had actually said that, in complete sincerity, I swallowed and answered that I was happy to see my family again soon, but that I was also sad to be leaving. I gave up, there was no point in trying to get through to her.

My dreaded last day at WEST arrived. I had everything packed and went to the children's homes to spend as much time as possible there, before I had to leave, at noon. For once – a rarity for me, when it comes to leaving places or starting new things – I was completely aware that I was about to go and leave this behind. I felt shaky all day and burst out in tears several times.

The person who was having the most difficult time with my leaving – as bad, or possibly worse than I myself – was Sun. The whole last week I was at WEST she would tear up regularly, though not allowing herself to actually start crying. Apart from leaving the children, saying goodbye to her was the hardest thing. What made it all worse was that I just did not know if I would ever see her again. The most frequently asked question in those days must have been 'Will you come back again?'. I just did not know and I did not want to make any promises that I was not sure I could keep. So I told everyone the difficult truth. That I hoped I would be able to come back again for a visit sometime, but that I did not know if I would be able to, because it is very expensive to do so. I would need to find a good job and save up first.

Before we left for the station, we had lunch together one last time: the shift supervisors, the cook Hai, Hua, Sun and I. The cook had made my favourite food, at my request, a noodle dish. After I had finished one bowl, all the people present took it in turn to get me another helping, which was being presented and received officially, with two hands. A terribly loving gesture. Even if it did mean I was close to exploding. Hua finally kindly said that she would not give me another serving, which I thanked her profusely for, bowing to her with my hands together before my chest. That in turn was appreciated very much too.

After lunch, I went to the children's homes one last time, saying goodbye from the threshold, in tears. All the *ayi* gathered around and said goodbye, many crying as well. First the baby home, then the toddler home. Then it was time to get into the car, which was already loaded with my bags.

Hua and Sun accompanied me to the station. There were no babies who needed to go to EAST, so for once I would be travelling without a baby, an unusual experience. There was an *ayi* coming with me, because there was a baby who needed to be brought back from EAST. At the station Sun once more showed her skills by getting us to the train the easier way, and getting herself and Hua onto the train without platform tickets, even though we did not have babies with us for leverage this time.

Once on the train the four of us sat two by two opposite each other, silently, desolately. Sun and I had our hands gripped together as if holding on for dear life. There was a shuffle, moving of bags, getting something, which was needed. Then we sat down again. This time Sun was next to me. After another minute or so, Hua proposed that there really was not much point in prolonging this further. Suddenly it became even more real, the fact that we were going to have to say goodbye.

Almost instantly, as if with one mind, Sun and I threw our arms around each other and cried on each other's shoulder. It is hard to say for how long. In the end Hua pulled us apart, the train would be leaving soon and they had to get off. I embraced and said goodbye to Hua, who had become good friend. One last hug with Sun and then she was lead away by Hua. While she walked away, our hands did not lose touch until the tips of our fingers really could not reach anymore.

I watched the two of them through the window as we were waiting for the train to start moving. Wondering if I would every get to see them again. If I would ever be able to come back here again. Tears rolled down my face. I was leaving one of the homes I have in the world, even if it was one I would not want to settle permanently in. I stood by the decision to leave, not to stay, I did not regret it or question it. But not now. Now was not the right time.

I slept a large part of the train journey. In the evening I arrived at EAST again. I still had three days left in China. Which of course I spent working. What else would I do? I had deliberately planned it so that I would have a few days left at EAST to give me a chance to say goodbye to the people and children there. However now that I was there and had left WEST, I found myself mainly waiting for the departure of the train. Having left WEST it felt to me like the real goodbye had been said. I was on my way out.

I did have a goodbye lunch with some people and a goodbye dinner with another set of people the day before I left, which was nice. Then an evening of frantic packing and organising. On the day of departure I had to leave at six in the morning. The medical director had gotten up to help me drag all my luggage downstairs to the car. One of the shift supervisors even brought me all the way into the train, on her day off.

There I was on the Transsiberian express, on my way home. I shared my cabin with three foreigners, so the Chinese adventure was broken off quite abruptly, which saddened me somewhat. Being on the train for almost 10 days, is not very adventurous, but it was a good opportunity for contemplation. Which is why I had chosen to return that way. To give me some time to get used to leaving China and the life I had there behind, before having to step into my European life again.

Epilogue

It seemed like a carefully thought out plan, to return by train, give myself time to process things and then be ready to take on life again, once I got off at the other end. It did not work quite as simply as that. When I got off the train, I was very happy to see my family again. I did not really experience culture shock as such, as everyone presumed I would, having to get used to things being so different from how I had experienced them for a year.

As a matter of fact, what I always find hardest, when returning from somewhere where I have experienced things which are really significant to me – and that goes just as much for coming back from France or Denmark as coming back from China – is how normal and natural it feels to be walking through the streets of my own country again. There is no sense of 'I have not been here for a year' or comparing it to where you came from. It is like a slot, which you fall into whether you want to or not. It just makes perfect sense to be walking there. It does not even feel like 'I am back'. It just feels like, 'I am here'. That can be quite disconcerting.

A larger 'adjustment-problem' was much vaguer, however. It took me quite a while to discover that it existed at all. At a certain point I realised that I was living in a kind of haze. I was happy to see family and friends again, but somehow I felt a distance between us, which neither they nor I put up. Also I felt like I did not have my mind on what I was doing. But this was not because I was preoccupied with China or with anything else. I was not aware of my mind being anywhere. So where was it?

It took me about a month to start to 'wake up'. To be more engaged in what I was doing and to be thinking more clearly. I am back just over two months now. Although I am participating in what is called 'normal life' again – having a job, looking for accommodation, writing – I would not claim to be all the way back yet. And I do not think I will ever go back to who I was before this year. Which is not a bad thing.

The year in China is by far the most fulfilling and worthwhile experience I have ever had in my life. I have learned so incredibly much, in so many ways. Language, practical skills, about China, about myself, you name it. Some of the things I am learning only now, looking back on it.

Even towards the end, when I was still in China, my goal when I returned to Europe was to try – once again – to get into freelance translating and earn my living from home. Making money translating and having time to do my writing. And then hopefully in time I would have a family, whom I would take care of and support. If possible getting in some travelling along the road.

Since I have come back, I am starting to feel more and more that such a 'sedate' life would not suit me anymore. I would still like to have the family. But I do not want the year in China to have been this great experience, which you spend the rest of your life telling your children and friends about. 'The time when I was alive.' I have learned too much there to just push it aside and leave it at that. I feel that I really have something to contribute and that I could learn so much more and add to what I have come to know.

I also know in the western world I am not allowed to use any of the skills I have learned in China, because I am not a certified nurse or doctor. I would absolutely love to learn more, in a practical hands-on way, with books on the side to read up on things as well. However I have no intention of going to medical school and come out a paediatrician in ten years time, by which time most of the fire I feel now about doing something real, will most likely have been put out.

So what I am thinking of doing now is to go on, in a small way. I have learned a lot not just about medical childcare, but also about institutional care, the places where things go wrong easily and babies fall through the cracks and ways in which these cracks can often be sealed relatively easily with few means. With this knowledge, I think I have something to contribute.

I want to travel to different developing countries, all of which have institutional care for infants, be it because babies are abandoned, or orphaned, and help out, learning and giving along the way. I think I have something to contribute.

Initially they will have to be intermittent projects. I will have to spend time working and saving, and then I can live off my savings for a while again. But that is all right. If that will enable me to do this. And maybe, in time, if I can manage to make a small difference, I might be able to access some grant or sponsorship to keep me going.

Of course this is only a tiny drop in the ocean. There are millions upon millions of children in the world living under horrible conditions. In China, our foundation took care of about 350 out of up to 20,000 abandoned children. When you look at it like that, it is nothing. But when you look at it from the perspective of those 350 individual children, it is a whole lot. Any single child, whom you can give a better quality of life, is a lot. So that is where I intend to start, with the little bits.

Acknowledgements

There are so many people to whom I owe a great debt of gratitude and unfortunately I cannot mention any of them by name. Still I'm determined to mention them.

    Large thanks of course to my parents for their understanding and support. Not many parents would find it in them when told their daughter is planning to go to China for a year to react by saying: That sounds like a great experience. Do you have any idea what you want to do there yet? And especially to my father for designing the cover for this book.

    Also to the rest of my family who with emails and packages of books showed me their support. And the two lovely ladies who took such good care of my during my stay in their B&B that I managed to write almost all of the first rough draft of this book in a few days time.

    Most of all, of course I have to thank the wonderful people I got to know in China. People who have taught me so much, have given me marvellous opportunities and support and great friendship. Particularly S.Y.L., N.J.H., Z.J.X., W.J.Y., L.L.J.,Z.L.P., A.K.,T.X., S.J., B.J., S.W., E.D., R.M.

    And all the babies who have let me care for them and who have taught me more than anyone, even I, can imagine.

March 2008

Comments are welcome at florentinekay@gmail.com

Medical Glossary

Anal Atresia: Also called imperforate anus. At birth the baby does not have an anus, so its bowels do not have any exit. Unless an exit is created soon after birth, the condition is fatal.

Cerebral Palsy: A form of brain damage which causes motor problems. This can take on several forms, spasticity, problems with balance and/or fine motor skills and compulsive incessant movement can be involved. Mental retardation may or may not be involved. Cerebral Palsy can occur before, during or after birth. It can not be cured and it is not progressive, so whatever damage is there, you need to live with.

Cleft lip/palate: During pregnancy part or all of the palate, yaw and upper lip fails to close. This can lead to anything from only a slight indentation in the lip, to a full, bilateral - under each nostril - cleft lip and palate, leaving the nose as the roof of the mouth.
In China the lip is corrected, when the baby reaches 3 months of age and its weight is 5kg. Once it has reached a year of age, it can also have palate surgery, which is a bigger operation. After this many children still need speech therapy and often dental work, at a later age.

Clubbed Feet: During pregnancy one or both feet were turned inward – in varying degrees – causing tendons and muscles to shorten so as not to allow the feet to be brought into a normal position by gentle handling.

Using the Ponsetti method by a series of plaster casts, the position of the foot is changed bit by bit, allowing tendons and muscles to stretch. When the foot is almost back to normal position, the Achilles tendon is severed, through a slight incision - this part we had done by a doctor -, and the foot is cast again in proper position. After three weeks the cast is removed and the tendon has re-grown, longer. Then the baby is made to wear an abduction brace – little shoes in a certain position on a metal bar – 23 hours a day for three months and after that 12-14 hours, while sleeping, until he or she is 4 years old.

Most children learn to walk normally once their feet are back in the right position.

Dysphagia: Neural damage in the brain causes loss of control of the muscles in the mouth. This can lead to anything from difficulty to impossibility of eating and swallowing, as well as speech. In many cases in children it is non-degenerative, depending on the cause.

Epilepsy A seizure disorder which comes from neural damage, which can have different causes. Seizures can comprise anything from slight twitching, momentary absence to complete rigidity of all muscles, violent lashing out of limbs, and even stopping breathing, leading to oxygen deprivation. Often seizure disorders can be controlled with anti-convulsive medication, but it is not always possible to bring the condition under control.

Hydrocephalus: The spinal fluid which flows into the brain, is not – or not entirely – re-absorbed. As the fluid accumulates, it causes pressure to build up in the brain and over time the head will start expanding. Unless something is done to relieve the pressure, the condition can lead to severe brain damage and can be fatal. Unfortunately the different possible treatments all involve high risk.

Pierre-Robin Sequence: During pregnancy for unknown reasons the foetuses lower jaw grows insufficiently. This leaves the tongue with too little room to grow. In order to make room, the palate is unlikely to close, leaving it cleft. The tongue tends to grow too far to the back of the mouth and after birth has a tendency to slide back into the throat, blocking the airway. Airways can also be more narrow than normal. All of which combined causes potentially lethal breathing problems.

Only the baby's growth can cause the airways to get wider. Until that time, the baby needs to be held prone at all times to prevent breathing problems as much as possible. The palate is not generally repaired until other problems have resolved, since this could cause further breathing difficulties.

Prematurity: Birth after a gestation of less than 37 weeks is considered premature. The shorter the gestation, the more likely problems are to occur. Common problems include: low birth-weight, apnoeic spells - breathing stops and/or heart rate drops -, instable body temperature, feeding problems, and higher risk of infection. The individual problems need to be dealt with to allow the baby to grow bigger and stronger.

Spina Bifida: During pregnancy the baby's spinal column failed to close, leaving nerves within it exposed – though usually still covered by skin. In some cases the baby has a bag on its back, in which spinal fluid accumulates. This needs to be removed, as it will continue to grow and in all likelihood eventually rupture, which leads to infections that are usually fatal.

If the bag is removed successfully, the prognosis depends on the original position of the bag. The lower the bag was on the back, the higher the chance of permanent problems. Including possible paralysis of the legs when the bag is at the base of the spine.

Bibliography

Johnson, Kay Ann.
> *Wanting a Daughter, Needing a Son. Abandonment, Adoption and Orphanage Care in China.* Yeong & Yeong Book Company. St.Paul, Minnesota 2004

Mosher, Steven W.
> *A Mother's Ordeal. One Woman's Fight Against China's One-Child Policy* Park Press. New York 1993

Zhai Shengde. Ed. Buschkens, W.F.L. & Platenkamp, J.D.M.
> *Studies on China's Contemporary Social Structure.* Drukkerij F.S.W. Leiden 1991